CONTENTS

Author's Note

The title of our Course is 'The Nineteenth-century Novel and its Legacy'; and now that the moment has come to look back on the Course, there are two very general questions which we might ask ourselves. The first is, what *is* the nineteenth-century novel—that is to say, what, if anything, can you say about it in general? And the second is, what was its legacy? So I shall make these the two main headings of this final Unit.

In the course of writing the Unit I have talked a good deal with the rest of the Course Team, especially Arnold Kettle and Graham Martin, and here and there you will find an exchange of view between us. This should remind you, if a reminder is necessary, that there is not meant to be anything authoritative about my own account of things.

Arts: A Third Level Course

The Nineteenth Century Novel and its Legacy Unit 32

Legacies

Prepared by P. N. Furbank
for the Course Team

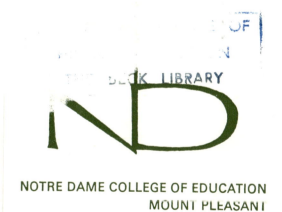
The Open University Press

The Open University Press
Walton Hall Milton Keynes

First published 1973.

Designed by the Media Development Group of the Open University.

Printed in Great Britain by
Martin Cadbury Printing Group, a division of Santype International.

ISBN 0 335 00832 1

This text forms part of an Open University course. The complete list of units in the course appears at the end of this text.

For general availability of supporting material referred to in this text, please write to the Director of Marketing, The Open University, P.O. Box 81, Walton Hall, Milton Keynes, MK7 6AA.

Further information on Open University courses may be obtained from the Admissions Office, The Open University, P.O. Box 48, Walton Hall, Milton Keynes, MK7 6AA.

1.1

1.0 THE NINETEENTH-CENTURY NOVEL

shall deal with this under four headings: *Fictional Conventions; The 'Moral-decision' Novel; 'Jude' and the 1890s;* and The *'Three-decker'*.

1.1 Fictional Conventions

Before going any further I would like you to re-read the opening chapter of *Middlemarch* and of *On the Eve*.

These chapters are both brilliant pieces of novel-writing, I think you will agree, and not altogether unlike. They both launch you, with comparatively little preparation, into a dialogue between two major characters, in the course of which you learn a good deal about the two as personalities and a certain amount about their history and situation, and are introduced—by means of the contrast between the two—to an important moral theme in the novel. And as well as this you have been entertained with a little 'scene', in the theatrical sense (more obviously so in *Middlemarch*, perhaps, than in *On the Eve*). There are obvious differences between the passages, too. Turgenev is far nimbler, more glacing and economical, in his effects than George Eliot. But it is the likenesses that interest me here, and I think they extend much further than I have suggested so far. The two chapters are very different, technically speaking, from any likely to have been written in the eighteenth century. One has the sense of a long tradition behind these chapters. The authors, one feels, are drawing on a vast range of accepted fictional devices, an inherited repertoire which has become second nature to them. It seems the naturalest possible thing to write a novel in this fashion; but that is only because we are conditioned to it. So I want you to stand back from it for a moment and see what a highly conventionalised and artificial affair it is.

If you will examine that chapter by George Eliot you will find that she is doing a whole succession of different things in it. First, she gives you a physical and moral description of Dorothea; then an exposition of some facts about Dorothea's family life; then a character-comparison with Celia—mixed up with general observations on life, historical reflections, and mock-addresses to the reader ('And how should Dorothea not marry?—a girl so handsome and with such prospects?'); then a scrap of narrative ('Sir James was going to dine at the Grange today . . .'); then a little dramatic scene, with dialogue (the jewel-scene); then an omniscient dive into Celia's private consciousness; and finally another clinching scrap of dialogue.

If you were ever tempted to think of the novel as simply 'holding up a mirror to life', you would have to admit, in face of this, that it is a much more complicated piece of apparatus than a mirror. And if you study the opening chapter of *On the Eve*, you will find the mixture of methods, and the transitions between them, even more marked: Turgenev moves incessantly around his two young men, describing, commenting, dramatising, giving stage directions, and finally producing a very expressive cinematic 'shot' of the rear view of the two protagonists against the landscape.

It is, in both cases, quite a collection of different devices, yet you do not notice them as devices. You do not have any awareness of the joins and transitions between one kind of approach and another—partly because the authors are so expert in disguising the joins and in giving the whole thing a rhythm and flow, and partly because you are so familiar with the method anyway. The word to catch hold of, I think, is 'rhythm'. Rhythm has to do with time; and this whole method of novel-writing has a definite purpose and function, closely bound up with time. Somewhere about the end of the eighteenth century, novelists began to be much more concerned with time, the time in which human events occur, and began to imitate and mimic time in a way that earlier novelists, and writers of epics and sagas (see Unit 23), did not attempt. There is a passage in Homer's *Odyssey* in which Ulysses, after his twenty years of wandering, has returned home to Ithaca. He has come back *incognito*, but his old nurse, who is washing his feet, recognises a childhood scar of his and is about to cry out, when he clutches her by the throat to restrain her. It is one of the great emotional climaxes of the story; but at this very point Homer interrupts his narrative for seventy lines to tell us how Ulysses got the scar. Now, you might think Homer was trying to create suspense, but this is plainly not the explanation; the digression does not follow the natural rhythm of suspense, and indeed 'suspense' as an artistic notion is something that has probably never entered Homer's mind.[1]

For the nineteenth-century novelist, on the other hand, suspense (which is to do with the rhythms of human time) is part of his regular stock-in-trade. Digressions for him are not *just* digressions (as they still are, on the whole, for eighteenth-century novelists). The time taken up by digressions—reflections, character descriptions, exposition, etc.—has, for him, an understood relation to the pace of events and helps in depicting that pace. It is a form of mimicry of time and has grown so habitual that novels from an earlier period, where the trick had not yet become so established, look old-fashioned, like painting before perspective.

Now this habit of imitating the flow and rhythm of time has itself a further human and artistic purpose. Its function is to persuade the reader that, by the end of a novel, he has himself lived through a certain amount of life. I have referred to moral reflections, character descriptions, exposition and so on as 'digressions', by which I mean that they are static and do not directly advance the story. It is perhaps not a very strict use of the word, since at that rate half or more than half of most novels would be 'digression'; but if you allow me the word, it will help to bring out an important fact, which is that digression is absolutely fundamental to the nineteenth-century novel.

For, as I have said, one of the things that all nineteenth-century novels are doing, to a lesser or greater extent, is giving the reader the feeling that he has enjoyed some days of vicarious living. And whereas the characters in the novel live their lives at a continuous pitch of intensity, the reader has to be given relief; as well as his shocks and dramas he must have his lulls and distractions, his periods of recuperation and aftermath. So the novelist, every now and then, moralises to the reader, or takes him on a round of visits or on a walk, or puts him to bed: he has to look after the reader's health in this way. Or again, from time to time, the novelist may make one of his characters look out of a window, or may do so himself. For a moment, we watch the general current of life going on, before plunging back into our particular drama. Likewise, again—this is a favourite effect—the novelist may *re-introduce* us to one of his central characters. We may run up against this character by chance somewhere and have his appearance described to us as if he were quite a stranger. Here, for instance, is Hardy using the device in *Jude the Obscure*:

[1] I have taken this example from *Mimesis: the Representation of Reality in Western Literature* by Eric Auerbach.

It was the spring fair at Kennetbridge, and though this ancient trade-meeting had much dwindled from its dimensions of former times, the long straight street of the borough presented a lively scene about midday. At this hour a light trap, among other vehicles, was driven into the town by the north road, and up to the door of a temperance inn. There alighted two women, one the driver, an ordinary country person, the other a finely built figure in the deep mourning of a widow. Her sombre suit, of pronounced cut, caused her to appear a little out of place in the medley and bustle of a provincial fair.

And who is this handsome-looking widow? Well, of course, it's our old friend Arabella. But the moment of doubt creates a powerful illusion. If it takes us a moment to recognise her, then—we irrationally feel—she *must* be real, and not just invented.

These pauses and fresh starts in the narrative have the effect of distancing the events before them and allowing memory to play round them, as if they were real events. They begin to have the remoteness and appeal of our own irretrievable past. And all the more is this so, since the reader has probably lived some of his own life between reading one chapter, or one volume, and the next.

Now, what do we feel about this whole aim and procedure of the nineteenth-century novel? Consider, that we speak of the nineteenth-century novel as 'realistic'; and rightly, in a sense; for Mr Brooke in *Middlemarch* seems 'just like life'—we have often met people like him; and the houses and furniture and bodies seem solid and recognisable; we do not feel, as we often do with twentieth-century novelists, that we are not sure what is real and what is not, or what 'reality' is. Yet when we think of 'realism', we tend to associate it with truth; whereas what is nineteenth-century realism doing, at least as you find it in George Eliot and Turgenev, but fostering a lie and an illusion, the illusion that you as a reader have lived some days at the novelist's expense?

This is not an idle question. It is one which, in the later years of the century, novelists themselves began to ask. They grew dissatisfied with that method I described earlier, by which the novelist, as you might say, did what he liked—described, expounded, confided, reflected, dramatised, told you the character's private thoughts or pretended to be ignorant of them—as the fancy pleased him. It seemed to them too impure, too much of a confidence trick. In order to produce the illusion in the reader that reading a novel was itself a kind of living, the novelist, they felt, had to falsify life: he used his privileges as a novelist to make life out more 'real', more recognisable, more reassuringly familiar than it really is. They felt that the time had come to make more rules for themselves. The novelist, they considered, must separate out the various devices at his command and not practise them all at once, as George Eliot and Turgenev do. If he is describing a character 'from the outside', he should not cheat and report his inner thoughts. If, like Conrad in *Heart of Darkness*, his subject is a particular man, Marlow, telling a story to a particular audience, a man struggling to get to the bottom of a baffling experience but knowing, too, that he will never be able to communicate half that he feels, then the writer should stick to this subject strictly, not lapse into some routine story-telling procedure. Or if, like Virginia Woolf in *Mrs Dalloway*, he is interested in the *moment*, the peculiar quality of instantaneous experience, he should limit himself to this focus, not combine this angle of vision with others.

Joyce, in *Ulysses*, went so far in separating out the various techniques of the novelist (as well as inventing various new ones of his own) that each section of his novel is written according to a different technique; and one of the purposes of his novel was to show up the mixed method of the nineteenth-century novel as the confidence trick that it was. Reading 'modernist' novelists like Joyce and Virginia Woolf becomes a different experience from reading nineteenth-century fiction. The old, conventional narrative rhythm, with its dramas and lulls, its suspense and its aftermaths, its pauses for reminiscence, and endings that are like death-beds where every word counts for twice as much: this rhythm was abandoned, and with it the comfortable illusion of enjoying some days of vicarious living.

GRAHAM MARTIN: It seems to me that there may also be a general problem here—the relation of 'art' and 'reality' in any period. One cultural period accepts as 'natural' the ways its novelists and painters represent 'reality', yet the next age often criticises precisely these ways for being 'artificial'. The strangeness and difficulty of new art often arises less from inherent obscurity than from its challenge to reigning conventions, and determinations to create new ones. Joyce and Woolf claimed that their 'fiction' represented 'reality' more faithfully than their predecessors, yet if we look carefully we can see how much of that 'reality' is actually being defined—rather than reflected—by new artistic conventions. Thus, they play down 'story' because it imposes what seems to them a false shape on experience. But their fictional methods impose other assumptions. Joyce's world is 'circular', repetitive, because he has little place for the kind of purposive action that changes things, or for stable, valued achievements. Woolf's undermines the assumption that social structures, or institutions, can give meaning to life: only individual acts of creative insight can do that. These assumptions are not uncongenial to the modern mind, so that the novelistic methods that reflect them are bound to seem less 'artificial' than the methods of another century. Yet *assumptions* is what they are. What, maybe, is more peculiar to these twentieth-century novelists is their degree of sophistication. In one way, their novels are much more strenuously 'artistic', as if, built into them, is the determination to show that 'art' is *not* 'reality', and that the reader will not be allowed to forget that what he is reading is a novel, and not a slice of life.

1.2   The 'Moral-decision' Novel

I now want to draw your attention to another aspect of the nineteenth-century novel—this time one peculiar to English fiction. If you consider *Mansfield Park*, or *Middlemarch*, or *Great Expectations*, I think you may fairly say that, in each, the actions turns upon moral decisions. Take *Mansfield Park* for instance. Could one not say that, in a sense, everything leads up to and leads away from Fanny's decision not to accept Henry Crawford? Poor Fanny! She is a limited and unsophisticated girl, and the odds against her are so heavy. Everyone will think her a fool, or an ungrateful girl, for refusing Crawford: he is attractive and charming and delicate in his behaviour towards her; she is miserable at Portsmouth; and marriage to him would be a way out of all her difficulties. All she has to depend on, against this, is her moral instincts, which warn her to beware of Henry. In the earlier part of the novel we have watched the development of these instincts and seen what factors fostered them and what factors discouraged their growth. Now, with knowledge, fascination and anxiety, we see them in action, in the taking of a moral choice on which her whole future, even her salvation, depend.

Wouldn't it be true, too, to say that the true climax of Dorothea's story in *Middlemarch* is the moment when, having already survived one shattering blow to her faith in life, by dint of living for others, she goes to visit the Lydgates, on an altruistic errand, only to receive an even more devastating blow—Will, who she thought needed her faith and love, is apparently having a cheap affair with Lydgate's wife. It is her ultimate moment of testing, to which all the rest of her career has led up. She has a choice—not a purely rational choice like Fanny's in *Mansfield Park*, but a crucial one none the less. It is whether, at this low point of her fortunes, she shall think of herself, which may mean despairing of life, or shall think of others. As you know, after a night of self-questioning, she opts for the second course: she goes out to try to 'save' Rosamond, and in doing so saves herself. Barbara Hardy has some good remarks on this subject, which you should look at, in her comparison between *Middlemarch* and *Anna Karenina* in Unit 26 (pp. 66). She says:

In George Eliot and Henry James, for all the subtlety of their particulars, there is a basic sheep and goats division. George Eliot in *Middlemarch*, for instance, is applying a fundamental moral test—are the people acting from self-interest or from love? The novel raises the question, and it is not possible to answer it crudely, but at the end of the action we can give a fairly satisfactory answer, and never have to reply 'Don't know'.

Think again of *Great Expectations*. Surely the climax of Pip's story is the return of Magwitch, and the testing of Pip which this represents. Everything else is a preparation for this moment of testing. What will Pip do in the face of this crushing blow to all his assumptions and golden expectations? Can he come to terms with it at all? Will he, for instance, try to deny Magwitch's claim on him altogether? All the influences for good in his character (like Joe) and all the influences for evil (like Miss Havisham) will have played their part in the answer; and the upshot—very convincing to us—is that, on balance, Pip 'saves' himself, but emerges permanently crippled and diminished.

You may say that I am reducing complex fictional masterpieces to the status of 'improving tales'; but I would answer that, at bottom, that is what they are. The novels of Jane Austen, George Eliot and Dickens are didactic, evangelical, 'improving' (though remember Graham Martin's discussion of the word 'didactic' as applied to George Eliot in paragraph 2.2 of Units 13–15). These novels are written to do you good. The authors say: 'I will show you, for your own good, the moral law in action, and how all a man's life may be a preparation for a choice on which salvation or damnation depends'. Typically—though of course not invariably—nineteenth-century English novels show you their protagonists first of all as children, forming habits and tendencies, and then they rise to a climax, or climaxes, in which, suddenly, we see the full implications of these childhood choices and decisions. For these writers the true and proper subject of fiction is character formation. Here they are in line with Victorian opinion generally. Moralists like Carlyle or Thomas Arnold attached the same supreme importance to character and character formation; and even so eccentric a Victorian as Lewis Carroll could insist that 'the true object of life is the development of character'.

The word 'character' has a distinctively moral ring for Victorian writers and is not just a synonym for 'personality'. And one might go so far as to say that 'character', in their sense, is for them the supreme reality and all other aspects of existence—physical experience, economic conditions and so on—are only significant in so far as they influence character. I do not mean that the Victorian novelists took a crude or rigid view of character: on the contrary. You may remember that remark of Mr Farebrother's in Chapter 72 of *Middlemarch*:

'But my dear Mrs Casaubon . . . character is not cut in marble—it is not something solid and unalterable. It is something living and changing, and may become diseased as our bodies do.'

This expresses George Eliot's own attitude very well, and it is true also of Jane Austen and, to a degree, of Dickens (Dickens alternates between this and a more fatalistic view of character). And I do not mean that it is any limitation on the novelists' range of curiosity: George Eliot and Dickens are as wide in their interests as Balzac or Tolstoy.

Nevertheless, the fact does constitute a major difference between nineteenth-century English novelists and their French and Russian counterparts, and marks the English novel out as a special product of Protestant culture. Novelists like Balzac and Tolstoy are fully as much moralists as George Eliot or Dickens, and innumerable sermons might be based upon *Cousin Bette* or *Anna Karenina*, but the books themselves are not sermons, and that is what *Middlemarch* and *Great Expectations* are. They depend on the reader's anxiously and personally involving himself in the characters' 'testing' or trial and—supposedly—being 'improved' in the process.

You can see this fictional tradition surviving in E. M. Forster (and indeed in plenty of novels today); and in this respect Forster can be seen as a Victorian novelist—in other respects he is less so. In Henry James, I think, you can see something else: the continental and the English traditions combining. James was greatly influenced both by Balzac and George Eliot, and *What Maisie Knew* seems at certain moments to be a 'moral-decision' novel and at other moments a dispassionate and Balzac-like depiction of a society red in tooth and claw. This is part of its strength.

Finally, I might mention *Huckleberry Finn*. You might expect me to quote this as a pure example of the 'moral decision' novel. For, certainly it leads up to a very memorable scene of moral decision: I mean the one in which Huck prays for the 'virtue' and strength of mind to hand Jim back to his owner, but finds it can't be done, and decides he had better take up 'wickedness' again—'which was in my line, being brung up to it'.

I took it [his letter to Jim's owner] up, and held it in my hand. I was a-trembling, because I'd got to decide, forever, betwixt two things, and I knowed it. I studied a minute, sort of holding my breath, and then says to myself:

'All right, then, I'll *go* to hell'—and tore it up.

This is a 'testing', all right, and a major event in the book. Yet *Huckleberry Finn* is not quite the sort of novel I am talking about, nor organised in the same way, and for this reason: Huck is too complete a hero. We never doubt for a moment that Huck will come out well from a moral crisis. The excitement in this scene lies not in doubting the outcome but in witnessing such an epic act of moral courage and single-handed overturning of conventional values. (Of course. I don't mean that Huck's decision-scene isn't full of tension, merely that the tension is of a different kind. It is the tension of irony—the irony that we, supposing us a nineteenth-century Southern reader, have been unsuspectingly led into trusting Huck's instincts and thus are now trapped into overthrowing all our most cherished prejudices.)

ARNOLD KETTLE: This point about Huck seems to me very true and interesting and accords with my reading of Elena's decision to marry Insarov in *On the Eve*, where, again, I get the sense of 'an epic act of moral courage' rather than the sort of moral decision about which the reader hovers, sharing the qualms and tensions of the characters concerned. One might also think of examples from *Wuthering Heights* and *Germinal*. The 'change' that comes over Heathcliff in the last chapters of *Wuthering Heights* clearly involves a moral struggle and a moral decision on his part, yet we don't, I think, see it in quite the same terms as the moral decisions in Jane Austen or Dickens or George Eliot: the reader doesn't assess the moral pros and cons in the same way.

Again, if one looks at Zola's treatment of Souvarine's action in destroying the mine and the conflict in his mind when he meets Etienne and realises that his friend will probably be killed through his action, I don't think the method of the 'moral-decision' novel is used. Souvarine's moral dilemma is described (p. 437) and we are told that he is deeply troubled. We are certainly given a glimpse of Souvarine's moral desperation; but we aren't as readers involved in his decision in the same way that we're involved in Pip's or Fanny's decisions.

Now I don't think this is simply because Souvarine is a fanatic or Heathcliff a monster or Elena an unusually determined girl. The difference from the 'moral-decision' novel that we sense in *Huckleberry Finn* and *Wuthering Heights* and *On the Eve* and *Germinal* doesn't imply that moral issues aren't at stake or that those moral issues are less vital than the one which, say, George Eliot poses. The difference, I think, is that in the non-English novels and in *Wuthering Heights* we encounter an element that's best called 'revolutionary'. Huck and Heathcliff and Elena and Souvarine are all caught up in situations in which the moral decisions they feel they must make are not covered by the accepted social morality of their societies, however rigorously and sensitively interpreted. Huck and Heathcliff, Elena and Souvarine are all involved in decisions which, whether right or wrong, take them outside the moral norms within which nineteenth-century society operates. They feel themselves forced to break through to an alternative morality. Both Huck and Heathcliff are literally prepared to go to hell. The structure of thinking and feeling which will contain the novels we can justly call 'moral-decision' novels simply won't hold the problems into which Mark Twain, Emily Brontë, Turgenev and Zola delve. (Whether it will hold Jude, the defeated rebel, is a question worth considering. What do you think?)

Putting it a bit crudely, I'm suggesting that the 'moral-decision' novel of the nineteenth century, with its sense of a close identity between the writer's and the reader's moral values and its posing of *limited* moral issues, can only work when the novelist basically accepts, with whatever reservations and criticisms, the bourgeois moral order. The more 'revolutionary' writers have to find other ways of engaging their readers' moral sympathies. But of course I *am* putting it crudely, for a division of our novelists into the conservative and the revolutionary poses as many problems as it solves, and one would certainly need to make many qualifications before accepting such a statement as 'Dickens was a conservative novelist, Turgenev a revolutionary one.' It's worth thinking about though.

GRAHAM MARTIN: I don't think I'm convinced that the 'moral decision' is so central as this. Isn't it a bit of a formula, like those governing Shakespeare's plays, that lets the novelists explore more interesting matters? Obviously, in one part of their thinking, Dickens, George Eliot, Jane Austen, Henry James (?) take moral decisions seriously enough, and they do greatly influence the narrative pattern. But the substance of their novels surely lies elsewhere. Aren't they even more interested in the ways people try to dodge moral issues, in the external pressures and internal self-deceptions that the whole business of 'morality' imposes on human nature? Perhaps what I mean is that there's a nineteenth-century element in those novels—'the moral decision'—that it's useful to be aware of, but that it doesn't reflect the novel's present claim to serious attention. I think that a twentieth-century reader is likely to find something parochial and over-simple in the kinds of moral decision that these writers worry about. This would suggest that the difference between the two centuries lies not so much in the emphasis on moral issues as in their contrasting conceptions of morality.

1.3 'Jude' and the 1890s

This final stage of the course is obviously the right one at which to look back over the nineteenth-century novels you have studied and consider how the novel changed over the century, and why. However, Arnold Kettle has already twice discussed this question of change and development—once from the vantage-point of the middle of the century (Unit 12) and again from that of its later years (Unit 23)—and has suggested plenty of lines of thought. So I won't go over the same ground myself. What I would like is to add one or two remarks, from a slightly different angle, about the later part of the period—mainly, really, to provide a background for *Jude the Obscure*.

The general point I want to make is that the mid-Victorian novelist, though he may be a bitter critic of particular aspects of the society he lives in, feels a special kind of responsibility for society as whole. At the deepest level, a novelist like Dickens or George Eliot reveres social order and authority and feels it important, even desperately important, to protect and preserve the social bond; and when he criticises particular institutions, it is for that very reason that he does so. When we come to the end of the century, however, the situation has changed; writers no longer feel this kind of responsibility, or not to the same extent. This fact seems to me helpful in understanding *Jude the Obscure* and putting it in perspective.

To explain what I mean I shall have to make an excursus into history, which I hope won't seem too much of a digression.

In thinking about the changes in Britain in the later part of the nineteenth century one useful thread to take hold of is *philanthropy*. Britain, with its missionaries and its anti-slave-trade campaign, was already in the pre-Victorian period the home of philanthropy, but in the mid-century philanthropy took a new impetus. With the failure of Chartism and the temporary defeat of socialism in Britain, and with, further (in 1848), the spectacle of violent revolution and reaction on the continent, the upper-middle-classes in Britain made a concerted effort towards reconciliation with the working-classes. This was the age of Christian Socialism and the founding of the Working Men's College, of fervent and paternalistic efforts to bring the benefits of culture to the working poor. Leading intellectuals, like Carlyle, Ruskin and Matthew Arnold, felt a peculiar kind of responsibility for English society, and novelists like Dickens and George Eliot shared this feeling. They felt that they were taking over, in this respect, from the Church and the aristocracy. And their influence was strong in the leisured classes generally. George Eliot's Dorothea, with her passion for putting her money and energy and feeling to wider social purpose, is a figure more characteristic of the 1850s than of the 1830s where George Eliot places her.

This tradition of unwearied and high-minded 'do-goodism' became incarnated in Gladstonian Liberalism, and it survived with some vigour at least until the 1914–18 war. Nevertheless, by the 1880s its heyday was over. For one thing, labour had once again succeeded in organising itself politically. For another, the educational scene had changed; there was compulsory primary education (1870), there were by now provincial universities (e.g. Manchester, 1880; Liverpool, 1884; Leeds, 1887)—so that the ambitions of Hardy's Jude, as Hardy himself says, wouldn't have been so hopelessly delusive had he been born then and not a generation earlier. Again, there had been drastic reforms of the army and the civil service. They now no longer functioned, or not to the same extent, on the old patronage basis and offered a 'career open to talents'. So did business, on an ever-increasing scale, and so did the civil service of the new Empire, which began quickly to expand in the 1880s. If the society of the 1840s was a more 'open' one than that of Jane Austen's day (see Unit 12), the society of the 1880s was considerably more 'open' even than that.

There was, further, a vast and growing suburban population (for instance the gigantic sprawling city south of the Thames), which did not fit into the neat world-view—Country and City; Church and State; Upper and Lower Class —of mid-Victorian thinkers and philanthropists. Everyone defined the 'suburbs' and 'suburban' differently, and almost everyone used the words as terms of abuse, but in fact, the suburbs were the nursery of the coming Britain and the source of most of its talent and energy. And, as publishers discovered, the suburban intellectual tended to be more open to ideas—ideas of every kind: Darwinian, Ibsenite, Shavian, etc.—than was the routine, classics-trained product of public school and university.

My point in this hopelessly hasty sketch is that the social and intellectual scene had become greatly diversified since the 1850s and less congenial to paternalistic philanthropy. It has become more of what we call a 'plural' society. And as a result you begin, in the 1880s and 1890s, to get a quite new kind of novel and play. This not only criticises the existing order of society, as Dickens did, but revalues the whole idea of society. In such works an individual will say, as it were, 'Let us stop making a mystery of Society and its authority. There is no infallible oracle, or Mount Sinai Tablet, or social contract, or body of elders, to tell us what is socially right. Society is *me*. I am society; or if I am not, I don't know who or what society is. And, after due thought, I hereby disown such-and-such an institution, as at present constituted, and set up another in its place. I here and now set up (say) the institution of companionate marriage without benefit of clergy. I hope others will follow me.'

This is the note of Ibsen and of Shaw and of Samuel Butler's *The Way of All Flesh* (written during the 1880s though not published till later), as later of D. H. Lawrence. These authors produced a new kind of work, one in which the hero tests and revalues all values for himself, and which aims to work on the reader, and make him revalue his values, in a direct and proselytising way. They are forward-looking works in a declared and committed way in which, on the whole, the great Victorian novels are not. And one of them, I suggest, is *Jude the Obscure*.

For this reason, my answer to Arnold Kettle's question about Jude on page 11— i.e. whether the 'moral-decision' novel can 'hold' Jude, the defeated rebel— would be 'no'. Though the novel is littered with moral decisions (few novels more so), it does not strike me as a 'moral-decision' novel in the sense we were discussing.

1.4   The 'Three-decker'

One solid reason for regarding the end of the nineteenth-century as a turning-point for English fiction, as we have done in this course, is that an important change in publishing methods took place at this time—to be precise, in 1894. This change was the disappearance of the three-volume novel (or 'three-decker'), and all that went with it. From the 1820s, novel publishing in Britain was ruled by a fairly strict convention, according to which a novel made its first appearance in book form in three volumes at a price of 10/6d a volume. George Eliot, the Brontës, Hardy and Henry James all came out in this way.

There were exceptions (the majority of Dickens's novels did not come out in this manner, for reasons connected with part-publication); but this was the rule, accepted as a matter of course by authors, publishers and readers. The convention also governed length: so that the publisher George Bentley in 1883 could tell an author that 'a novel consists of 920 pages with twenty one and a half lines on each page and nine and a half words in each line'. And it also to some extent governed content: as the century wore on, the accepted notion of a novel came to be a work which, in the words of a recent critic, 'reflected and magnified the conventional values of Queen, Church, Country and Family' and which 'allowed only the kind of complexity which could be generated by a twist in the plot or by a touch of villainy which in the end was rendered innocuous by poetic justice'. Kipling, who never wrote one, gave a valedictory salute to the 'three-decker' in 1894, describing it thus:

Full thirty foot she towered from waterline to rail.
It took a watch to steer her, and a week to shorten sail;
But, spite all modern notions, I've found her first and best—
The only certain packet for the Islands of the Blest.

Fair held the breeze behind us—'twas warm with lovers' prayers.
We'd stolen wills for ballast and a crew of missing heirs.
They shipped as Able Bastards till the Wicked Nurse confessed,
And they worked the old three-decker to the Islands of the Blest.

Needless to say, authors of the stature of George Eliot and Hardy did not simply pander to these conventional expectations: nevertheless they had to take them into account. They were hampered by them and frequently fretted against them; but on the other hand, as one should remember, they were in some respects given encouragement by them. A novel like *Middlemarch*, with its complicated and capacious structure—enabling it to take in such a wide sweep of English life—owes some of its inspiration to the three-decker convention (though actually, to be precise, *Middlemarch* came out in four volumes; and its publishing history was peculiar in other ways too, as Graham Martin explains in Units 13–15).

The three-decker was, or came to be, closely tied in with the circulating library. Even rich people could not afford all the novels they wanted at the inflated price of a guinea-and-a-half, and from the early 1850s Mudie's lending library, with its various imitators, came to be one of the main outlets for new fiction. The system suited publishers, for it meant they knew where they were: for the right literary product they had an assured market, of a known size, and could calculate their finances accordingly. In certain respects it suited authors too. The usual method of paying authors at this time was for the publisher to give them an outright sum for their copyright, or for so many years' hire of their copyright. For an author this plan had the disadvantage that if he wrote a best-seller the publisher reaped most of the benefit. On the other hand, like the publisher, he knew where he stood. If he produced a certain product, it had a certain definite market value. The Victorian novelist had a clearly-defined economic role, as member of a highly-systematised and rather old-fashioned and monopolistic industry.

I should remind you here that a novel by a popular author would, before appearing in book form at all, most probably have been published as a serial in a magazine, or—as was the case with many of Dickens's novels—in monthly parts. This, too, was a factor of much significance, though it is not my subject here, and you might find this a good moment to re-read what Graham Martin says about it, in section 4 of his Study Guide to *Great Expectations*.

As I have suggested, the three-decker system was not without its virtues. However, by the last decades of the century it had become, very plainly, an absurd anachronism. It was so on economic grounds: for with the development of cheap paper and the use of high-speed presses in book production, the guinea-and-a-half price was now out of all relation to manufacturing costs; and at the same time, as a result of compulsory education, the market for books—for books at a reasonable price—had grown and was growing enormously. And it was anachronistic on artistic grounds too: serious novelists, aware of Flaubert and Zola and of the intellectual esteem enjoyed by the novel in France, felt they could no longer submit to the censorship of Mudie's, nor bear to manufacture plot contrivances about wills and mistaken identity and long-lost relations. Also, they wished to experiment with the short novel, the 'novella' or 'nouvelle', which was much cultivated by serious writers in France (significantly, 'novelette', the equivalent term in English, still has a low-brow connotation). They felt it was intolerable that they should have to pad out their novels with long-winded conversations and meaningless incidents to fit them to the three-decker format.

There were protests against the three-decker system from many quarters during the 1880s, and one of them in particular, by the novelist George Moore, had some practical effect. In 1895 he trounced the circulating-library system, and the sort of sentimental novel it promoted, in a pamphlet called *Literature at Nurse, or Circulating Morals*, and in the same year he persuaded Vizetelly, Zola's English publisher, to issue his novel *A Mummer's Wife* in one volume, at a reasonable price. (Interestingly, the suggestion originated with Zola himself.) Other publishers followed Vizetelly's lead. So that when in 1894 Mudie's and W. H. Smith's—trying for greater profits—informed publishers that henceforth they would refuse to buy fiction for more than 4/- a volume, less discount, the publishers were in a position to retaliate. They had realised the growing possibilities of distribution as opposed to library circulation, and few of them accepted the libraries' ultimatum. As a result, the long-standing partnership between publishers and libraries came to an end, and with it the 'three-decker' and the censorship that the libraries had imposed upon fiction.

The results were complex. Serious novelists did gain the freedom they had demanded. Publishers became more willing to issue fiction of an unconventional kind—unconventional in length, in subject, in structure, in tone, and so on. (And the growth of the royalty system in paying authors—a development of the 1880s—encouraged this: for under this system, a publisher who doubted the commercial prospects of a book need offer only a very small advance on royalties.) One can sense the effects of the new freedom in Henry James's later work: the brevity, concentration and artistic rigorousness of *What Maisie Knew* are already a fruit of it, as are the speed, concision and originality of handling of *Where Angels Fear to Tread*. And, as I need hardly say, one cannot imagine such revolutionary work as Joyce's stories, or *Mrs Dalloway*, appearing in the age of the three-volume novel.

There were also losses, however. What for George Eliot had been merely a sense of a need for *distance* between the author and the life of his times (see Unit 23), grew, for the serious writer of the twentieth century, into a sense of positive isolation. He was up against the problem of a multiplication of standards. Let me explain that phrase. There had been a certain homogeneity of opinion in the Victorian reading public. The Mudie's subscriber would pay homage to the great names of literature, even if he didn't read them. The assumption was that there was only one standard in intellectual matters, and this standard was the perquisite of the educated upper classes. Part of the significance of the inflated price of the three-decker was that it gave a dignity, a respectability, to a form of literature considered, otherwise, as less 'serious' than history or philosophy. The difference between the Mudie's subscriber and the reader of 'railway novels' and 'penny dreadfuls' was felt, first and foremost, to be a social one.

The new development (or at least one of the new developments) in the situation of the 1890s was the notion that there might be a *variety* of intellectual standards: that one might *choose* to be a 'lowbrow' or a 'middlebrow'. Especially a 'middlebrow'. For one of the innovations accompanying the revolution in publishing methods was a systematic catering for the 'middlebrow' reader— the reader say, of Conan Doyle or, later, of John Buchan and Hugh Walpole. And the 'middlebrow' reader, for reasons deep in the changing nature of the English class-system, was ready to assert his independence in intellectual matters. He felt less compulsion to pay lip-service to 'classics' whom he had no intention of reading; and he would be inclined to pooh-pooh Joyce or Lawrence or Virginia Woolf as cranks or long-haired highbrows. Or he might not even have heard of them. With the growth of this 'middlebrow' reading-public, writers like Joyce or Lawrence or Virginia Woolf could no longer hope for national acceptance and honour on the same scale as enjoyed by Dickens or George Eliot.

2.0   THE LEGACY

2.1   Dealing with a Legacy

There are two things you can do with a legacy. One is to invest it prudently and live off the income; and this is how many twentieth-century novelists treated their inheritance from their predecessors. It is what Galsworthy and H. G. Wells did and what many quite interesting novelists are still doing today. Of course, they adapt the methods they have inherited to their own age: they abandon everything that is obviously anti-quated, all the long-windedness and dear foolish devices of the 'three-decker', together with explicit didacticism, and outmoded attitudes towards class and sex. They may use fiction expressly to attack the vices and crimes of the nineteenth century. Nonetheless their novels remain nineteenth-century novels in their underlying methods and artistic convention, and these—as has often been stressed in this course—are not merely a matter of technique but an expression of a particular ideology and a particular theory about the nature of reality. (Among those who use their legacy in this way I might also mention film-makers. The middle run of film-makers have regarded the nineteenth-century novel as their patrimony and have found ways of translating its devices into cinematic terms. In my view this has been a clog and an obstacle to the film's development as an art-form; but I can't pursue that here.)

There is a disadvantage in treating an artistic legacy in this way. It is the same disadvantage as with a financial legacy. Dividends drop, the currency becomes devalued, and the author, not being in a position to create new capital, finds himself living in reduced circumstance and genteel poverty. This is, broadly speaking, the situation of the traditional novelist today.

The other way of dealing with a legacy is to spend it, to 'burn' it, to squander it on some glorious and daring enterprise; and this is the course adopted by the more *avant-garde* of twentieth-century novelists—writers like Joyce and Virginia Woolf (and others, like Proust and Gide, who do not figure in this course). What I mean by their 'squandering' their legacy is that they wrote novels which, as well as being stories in their own right, were a running commentary on, and critique of, earlier methods of novel writing. You can see this in *Mrs Dalloway*. The novel, from one point of view, suggests a caricature of one of Dickens's sprawling London novels. It was a great discovery of Dickens's that coincidence, the stock-in-trade of every hack Victorian novelist, could actually be made a vivid expression of the lonely and mysterious nature of life in cities, where no one knows his neighbours and where the stranger passing you on the pavement may be the very man on whom your fate depends. However, in order to exploit coincidence, Dickens had to construct elaborate, and sometimes rather creaking, plot mechanisms. Virginia Woolf shows that a similar effect can be obtained with a fraction of the effort. She achieves all the artistic value of coincidence by certain formal unifying devices—by having the same features of her London day (the chimes of Big Ben, a closed car containing an important personage) experienced by a number of different and unrelated characters. In this she is taking a lesson from the plastic arts; it is the sort of 'compositional' device that is constantly used by painters.[1] And the point I want to make here is that the effortless facility of the procedure is felt by us as a sly comment on the cumbersomeness of the Victorian novel. (In point of fact she probably borrowed the idea from Joyce, who used it with more openly satirical purpose in *Ulysses*.)

In rather similar fashion Virginia Woolf 'sets up' stories or plots of a traditional kind—for instance the story of Peter Walsh's youthful love for Clarissa Dalloway—and then teases the reader by denying them their traditional development. 'Teases' is perhaps the wrong word; all I mean is that the reader, knowing his George Eliot and Dickens, cannot help forming expectations as to how such a story as this may develop (will seeing Clarissa again overturn Peter's life and make him give up his ideas of marriage?), and it is part of Virginia Woolf's intention that the reader should do so. Her novel is constructed out of the ruins of a traditional novel.

We must not think it was out of mere resentment or ingratitude that 'modernist' novelists squandered their legacy in this way. Joyce had a profound understanding of the nineteenth-century novel and was equipped to be a great master of it. And the same is true of D. H. Lawrence, whose first masterpiece, *Sons and Lovers*, was, broadly speaking, in the nineteenth-century tradition. One only has to read the opening pages of *The Fox* to realise what a master of traditional methods he is. In his confident, effortless-seeming manner he has established March and Banford—their characters, their history, their social background and their present relationship—with magnificent solidity. Here, even before Henry's arrival on the scene, are all the materials of a 'character' or 'moral-decision' novel in the George Eliot manner; and it comes as a subdued shock to us when the novel develops in a different manner—when we find that Lawrence has eventually switched our attention so far away from normal 'human interest' that Banford's removal from the story by murder becomes, not a climax, but a dream-like and almost insignificant event.

---

[1] Arnold Kettle goes into this question of Virginia Woolf's borrowings from the other arts in Unit 30. I will take the chance to add an example of my own. When, at two crucial moments in her novel, Virginia Woolf wants to express the flooding of tranquillity into the souls of Septimus Smith and Clarissa Dalloway, she boldly uses exactly the same words: 'Fear no more, says the heart . . .'. In this, it strikes me, she must have been consciously borrowing from music, where such repetitions of theme are normal. It is at such points that you feel the full distance Virginia Woolf has travelled from the traditional novel.

Virginia Woolf's relation to the tradition was somewhat different. For her, resentment did certainly enter in; she regarded the traditional novel as a 'man's' novel. (See Unit 30.) And it is not so plain how she would have fared as a traditional novelist. There is a certain thinness in the human material in her novels. It is, of course, all part of her scheme (what I have called 'constructing her novels out of the ruins of a traditional novel') that her minor characters, like Hugh Whitbread, should deliberately be presented as stock types and fictional clichés. But when it comes to a more important character, like Septimus's wife Lucrezia, one feels she would like to give her more solidity and individuality than she is quite able to.

2.2   Ceasing to Pamper the Reader

So much, for the moment, about the general nature of the 'legacy'. Let us now consider in more detail what the innovations of novelists like Joyce, Woolf or Lawrence consisted in, and what their purpose was. There is a general criticism you might make of the nineteenth-century novel: it may give a hard time to some of its characters, but it gives the reader an easy one. This is an important point, I think. It says much about the role of novels and novel reading in the nineteenth-century, and ultimately about the society which produced them. It was, at least, a point of significance for those who broke away from these traditions. I have tried to suggest earlier in this Unit (page 6) that most nineteenth-century novelists practised a certain kind of fictional rhythm, which imitates the rhythm of life as we all of us experience it: its suspense; its crises and aftermaths; its greetings and farewells and new starts; its pauses for recuperation; and its moments of retrospect. And I said, too, that this rhythm gave the reader the pleasant feeling of enjoying a period of life at the author's expense. My phrase about this was that the author was 'looking after the reader's health'—I might equally have said, his comfort. It was over this matter that twentieth-century novelists became most dissatisfied with the novel of the preceding century. They saw harm in the reader's being pampered and cossetted in this way.

One of the obvious differences between books and life—between reading about disaster or torture and witnessing them (let alone experiencing them) in real life—is that, in reading, you can always refuse to turn the next page. (Actually, when thinking about the relation of books to life, or reading to living, I think one should not ask oneself what the differences are, but what are the likenesses: they are really very few.) Someone reading a novel, then, is in a very comfortable position as compared with almost any other activity of his existence. But the nineteenth-century novelist is not satisfied with this. He takes all this extra care for the reader's comfort, tending the patient, and keeping him amused, with extreme solicitude;[1] and the consequence is that, to some eyes at least, the reader is altogether too well sheltered against the pains and shocks of life.

He is sheltered, and perhaps over-sheltered, in another way too: that is to say, against the idea of change. Nineteenth-century novelists have a way of setting their story a generation or so in the past, and this at once distances it and makes the reader feel less obliged to project himself into it in any active way. What is more important, these novelists are inclined to present events as the inevitable

---

[1] As just one example of the playful devices with which the Victorian novelist indulges the reader, think of the habit of telling the reader how characters will get on after the story closes. Even George Eliot allows herself to do this, though in rather a wry tone of voice.

result of certain 'laws' of psychology and human nature. (Think, for instance—as one random example—how George Eliot implies, in her portrayal of Lydgate, that there is a known law governing the psychology of doctors—or anyway of good doctors. The 'instinct of the healer' will exercise a certain definite and calculable effect, almost like a chemical reaction, on the pattern of their lives.) The reader may be touched or moved, but he has the author's backing in reassuring himself that, after all, things could not have been different. The nineteenth-century novelist, in setting up as a professional psychologist, is in a way denying human freedom and enouraging the reader to do likewise. Sartre puts this well in his attack on nineteenth-century fiction in *What is Literature?* (1950):

> In an ordered society which meditates upon its eternity and celebrates it with rites, a man evokes the phantom of a past disorder, makes it glitter, embellishes it with old-fashioned graces, and at the moment when he is about to cause uneasiness, dispels it with a wave of his magic wand and substitutes for it the eternal hierarchy of causes and laws

> (p. 106)

When I speak of the reader enjoying the illusion of living some days at the author's expense, you must understand that I don't mean his involving himself closely with the story, so closely that he reacts as he would in real life. I mean just the opposite; he enjoys the illusory days in a privileged state of freedom and immunity; he is living at the author's expense, not his own. In real life, especially where oneself or those whom one loves are concerned, one is far less inclined to accept the 'laws' of society and of psychology with resignation.

It is true that English novelists, writing the 'moral-decision' kind of novel, do try to interfere with the reader and involve him in a certain way, the way of 'improving' him—showing him an example of the ethical law in action, and engaging his sympathies for the actors in this imaginary case, so that he can profit from it in his own life. But this is a benefit the reader can take or refuse as he pleases. It leaves his freedom intact; and indeed 'involvement' is hardly the right word for it. It is also true that writers like Dickens and Zola sometimes make direct political appeals and challenges to the reader. Nevertheless, even with Dickens, the kind of 'life' that the reader enjoys at his expense is, we sometimes feel, one of impossible freedom and personal immunity. Indeed, what the nineteenth-century novel may be accused of covertly doing, by its 'confidence trick', is what Marx accused the bourgeoisie of doing in all its manifestations, i.e. passing off a man-made ideology as an immutable fact of nature.

It was upon this over-indulgence and pampering of the reader, which was so intrinsic a part of that familiar 'package', the nineteenth-century novel, that dissatisfaction centred among serious novelists at the end of the nineteenth-century. They saw it as their task to undo this 'package' and to submit each item in it to separate scrutiny.

2.3   The One-day Novel, etc.

One of these items was the device (see page 7) of playing on the reader's nostalgic tendencies, of making him, by various devices, look back on the events of a novel as though they belonged to his own past. To Joyce and Virginia Woolf it appeared illegitimate, and they found various ways of scotching it. One of these was to write 'one-day' novels—novels in which, since all the action takes place within twenty-four hours, there is no opening for sentimental memory.

I mention this particularly, because it was a very fruitful device and opened up a whole new field of activity, one very important to twentieth-century writers in general: I mean the focusing upon some *single* thing, scrutinising and magnifying it, like a drop of pond-water under a microscope, and extracting from it everything—the whole of a person's life, the whole life of Dublin, ultimately the whole world. In a sense, we feel we are getting the *whole* of Mrs Dalloway in Virginia Woolf's novel, and the whole, the complete epitome, of the hero in almost any of Joyce's short stories (his theory of 'epiphanies' is relevant here). And this getting-in of the whole is bound up with the concentrating rigorously on a single thing.

This quest for singleness and rigorous focus is important in modernist fiction and can take many forms. For instance, the prose of Mrs Dalloway is a *single* melodic line. Though varied with endless marvellous subtleties of rhythm and cadence, it is really one long sustained 'aria' (faintly recalling the soprano 'mad-scene' in an opera by Bellini or Donizetti). The thing is very different from the nineteenth-century novel, with its mixed assortment of ingredients, aimed at providing the reader with an elaborate mixed diet.

In Henry James, already, there is great stress on the need for this singleness and purity in conception and design. You may remember the quotation from his Preface to *The Spoils of Poynton*, in Miriam Allott's *Novelists on the Novel*:

> . . . most of the stories straining to shape under my hand have sprung from a single small seed, a seed as minute and wind-blown as that casual hint for *The Spoils of Poynton* dropped unwittingly by my neighbour, a mere floating particle in the stream of talk. What above all comes back to me with this reminiscence is the sense of the inveterate minuteness, on such happy occasions, of the precious particle—reduced, that is, to its mere fruitful essence.

When his neighbour at table goes on with the anecdote which has become his 'germ', he shuts his ears; he doesn't want to hear any more; his whole novel must unfold from that single seed.

2.4   Character

Another item scrutinised was 'character'. I tried earlier to suggest that, for a novelist like George Eliot or Dickens, 'character' and character-formation—character not just in the neutral sense of 'personality' but in a more ethical and moralistic sense, as when we praise someone for showing 'character'—represented the supreme reality, and all other aspects of existence were ultimately only significant, for them, in so far as they influenced character. It was not an absurd view of life but, as practised in the nineteenth-century novel, it tended to encourage a rather easy feeling of 'wisdom' on the reader's part, a comfortable acceptance of certain supposedly unchangeable 'laws' of human behaviour. To a novelist like D. H. Lawrence, obsessed with the creativeness of the human psyche, 'character' in the George Eliot sense seemed a cramping concept, and he felt the need, as a novelist, to dislodge it from its throne. You may remember his famous statement at the time of writing *The Rainbow*:

> You mustn't look in my novel for the old stable *ego*—of the character. There is another *ego*, according to whose action the individual is unrecognisable, and

passes through, as it were, allotropic states which it needs a deeper sense than any we've been used to exercise, to discover are states of the same single radically unchanged element.

One should bear in mind that Lawrence is speaking specifically as a novelist. We are not to think that he rejects the whole idea of 'character' as George Eliot conceived it; indeed, as *The Fox* shows, he was a masterly depicter of 'character' in just her sense. It was merely that he felt that to erect this into the supreme reality produced a false and imprisoning kind of fiction. And, of course, he already had the example of certain great continental writers, Dostoevsky especially, to show what unexplored areas of experience were open to a novelist less restricted by this obsession with 'character'.

2.5   The Narrator

We have seen the reader deprived of his indulgence in nostalgia and other such indulgences fostered by the novel's mimicry of time. We have also seen him deprived of the pleasure of easy wisdom and the comfortable acceptance of psychological 'law'. What also can he be deprived of? Well, for one thing, the friendly and reassuring companionship of the narrator. One reason that the nineteenth-century reader could enjoy himself in his illusory 'living' was that a hospitable narrator was there to make him at ease. That narrator is still there in *Where Angels Fear to Tread*, establishing a social relationship with us, amusing us, chiding us, telling us what to think and generally acting as master of ceremonies. He is there still in *The Fox*, but we are not so sure what to make of him: he has such a queer, ruthless, cheerful tone of voice, telling us not to get too much involved in pity and other such traditional feelings. We are not quite clear whether he is our friend. And when we come to Joyce and Virginia Woolf, he has gone, apparently, almost altogether. We are left alone and unaided, as readers, and have to puzzle out for ourselves what attitude to take to the things we are shown and why we are expected to be interested in them at all. This is what is called 'objectivity'—and much more like the way things are in our own life. The novelist not only makes no efforts to conciliate us, he positively expects to dominate us, to transform our consciousness. We have humbly to apply ourselves to his paragraphs, abandoning all hope of living a dreamy fantasy life at his expense. We examine the exact words he uses with anxious care, for, as we have no idea what is coming next, we cannot afford to ignore any clue he gives us. The twentieth-century novel thus sets a premium on language. It is the language of prose, not of poetry, but it demands the same closeness of attention as the language of poetry (and, as a matter of literary history, it influenced the language of contemporary poetry).

2.6   Ethical Standpoint

We find, also, that we do not know where we are ethically. Are we to admire Clarissa Dalloway, and rejoice at Henry Grenfel's victory over Banford and his success with March? Or shall we consider Mrs Dalloway an egotistic snob and Henry a rather empty and dangerous young man? Nineteenth-century novelists like Balzac and Zola pretend an implacable indifference at the spectacle of the lamb thrown to wolves, but we know well enough what they really feel, and the feelings they mean to inspire in us. With these twentieth-century novelists this is not so true. Sympathy, ours and the author's, comes and goes; it flickers;

and there is no firm attitude or agreed set of values for us to fall back upon. We, as readers, have to *work* as we never worked in the halcyon days of the nineteenth-century novel.[1] We have our nose to the grindstone and are engaged in a moment-by-moment, empirical, first-hand evaluation of life.

2.7   Story

There is something even more fundamental that the reader is deprived of, or at least given much less of than he is accustomed to, and that is *story*. Story does not disappear altogether in these novels by Joyce and Woolf, and indeed it would be a contradiction in terms to speak of fiction without story, but the pulse of narrative beats more slowly and faintly in them. Consider the 'Hades' section of Joyce's *Ulysses*. All the various elements in it—physical description, conversation, action, and Bloom's internal monologue—are woven into a single thread, which unreels steadily and monotonously, and apparently to no particular end or climax. The old narrative rhythm is gone, and with it the old unseen narrator saying, by implication, 'Let me describe the background to you'; 'Now here is a little "scene" for you'; 'Before we go on, I ought to explain something', etc., etc. Instead, everything unfolds according to the same rigid formula. We have no sense of transition when we pass from spoken to unspoken words or from speech to action; and if there are any highlights or moments of climax, we have to find them ourselves, the author is not going to help us. But, indeed, we realise early on that if we are going to enjoy these pages we shall have to interest ourselves more in what is happening at the very moment than in what is going to happen next. And what this amounts to really, is almost to say that there is no story.

I have spoken of the 'Hades' passage in rather a slighting way, which of course I do not mean, for these magnificent pages of Joyce's have a quality absent from any nineteenth-century novel—except perhaps one or two of Henry James's— I mean strict unity of design. In being so homogeneous, so single, so 'pure', Joyce's pages have a certain advantage over a chapter of a nineteenth-century novel, which will inevitably be a 'mixed assortment' of things. And this is not just formal and technical matter, for, on Joyce's part, it is all part of his ambition to get *everything* in and to show the unity of internal and external experience.

Nevertheless, much is lost by abandoning, or at least so severely economising on, 'story'. In a sense, story (or plot) is a more profound, as well as an older, discovery than any of the brilliant inventions of 'modernist' novelists. There are important areas of human experience that can only be expressed by story (just as there are some that can only be expressed by ritual). And Dickens, by devising such a plot as that of *Great Expectations*, may be influencing us at a deeper level than all the 'depth psychology' of Joyce. The virtues of story are innumerable, and one of them is that a good story—like that of Pip and Magwitch, or that of *Hamlet*—is inexhaustible. No matter how many times you tell it over to yourself, it does not stale, indeed it may actually accumulate meaning. Religions, which aim at permanence, base themselves on stories, because a story is something which does not wear out.[2]

---

[1] I'm exaggerating, of course. Stendhal, for instance, certainly did make the reader work. As Arnold Kettle remarked in Units 8–9, p. 62, in comparing Stendhal with Balzac: 'Stendhal's more dialectical presentation, his evolving of a style *based on* (not just absorbing) contradictions, his refusal to isolate his people even for an instant from their context, does undoubtedly give *Scarlet and Black* a wonderful "openness" . . . The reader is needed to complete a Stendhal novel: without the reader's active effort of comprehension it cannot spring fully to life.'

[2] A colleague comments: 'A very loaded sentence, for (a) a religion can't aim at anything, or base itself on anything, and (b) I doubt if a "myth" and "story", should be taken as synonymous.'

But on the other hand, story, as developed by the nineteenth-century novelists—where it is fleshed out with endless realistic detail and used to create an illusion of everyday life—has disadvantages too. If you are telling a tale in this manner, a great deal of what goes into it will have to be merely *instrumental*. In order to give you a further instalment of Jude's affair with Sue, Hardy has to explain how Jude took the train from Marygreen to Melchester, at such and such a time of day; and this is very boring information considered in itself. (I have chosen Hardy as my example here, because he felt the problem acutely and in consequence tends to give the details of matters like journeys with a despairing literalness.) Again, a nineteenth-century novelist, for the purposes of his plot ('plot' here begins to distinguish itself from 'story') may have to give you an incident, like Pip's sister's mysterious encounter with an unknown assailant, which you won't understand the point of till twenty chapters later. For the time being you have to store the incident away in your mind in a mechanical sort of way.

Now, if, as a novelist, you are not purveying story or plot in this way, or not to the same degree, you do not have the same need for these merely 'instrumental' or mechanical features. Everything in your novel can be there for its own sake. We feel this to be so of everything in the Joyce passage (as we do of everything in *Mrs Dalloway*). You may, at a first reading, ask yourself why *any* of it is there; for after all, nothing much seems to happen, and Bloom's thoughts are mostly quite as trivial as our own. But at least if any of it has a right to be there, it all has. In this sort of novel we feel it to become important, for its own sake, to know what sort of a physical event it is when the rim of a carriage-wheel grinds against the curbstone—important enough for Joyce to use such extraordinary art in rendering it. ('The felly harshed against the curbstone: stopped.') It is not just scenic description or the 'background' to characters' thoughts and actions; nor is it there just to give verisimilitude. It is there in its own right.

Virginia Woolf, also, had a vision of such a novel, one in which there should be nothing merely 'instrumental'—no railway timetables, no riddles to be solved twenty chapters later—and where everything should be there for its own sake. She describes it in her diary for January 1920:

I figure that the approach will be entirely different this time: no scaffolding; scarcely a brick to be seen . . .

She goes on to picture this future novel of hers as 'all crepuscular' but with 'the heart, the passion, everything as bright as fire in the mist'. And here, of course, she is aiming at something very different from Joyce, who is not crepuscular or tenuous but on the contrary very earthy, concrete and specific. But in wanting a novel without 'scaffolding' she is at one with him.

ARNOLD KETTLE: This change in the status of 'story' as an integral part of a novel seems to me to be connected with some very general changes in the way people saw the world and themselves. Up to the end of the nineteenth-century, I'd think, novelists stick to story as the basic element of a novel because they see their society as 'there' and people as creatures whose existence is above all meaningful as social beings within an established, though not necessarily static, order of things. The hero may *go* mad but he can never *be* mad. The novelists may have some axes to grind but they grind them in a specific time and place and even the most revolutionary of them make certain pretty basic assumptions: e.g. that you can confidently relate certain effects to certain causes and that the passage of time is real and straightforward.

Such assumptions are questioned by the 'new' writers of the twentieth century.

You cannot be sure in a novel by Kafka or Virginia Woolf who is mad and who is sane. To Conrad, as to Marlow, the essence of a tale or a situation seems to be not like the kernel of a nut (which is pretty tangibly 'central' and the kind of thing that provides the 'point' of a 'story'), but something more mysterious

'enveloping the tale which brought it out only as a glow brings out a haze, in the likeness of one of these misty halos that sometimes are made visible by the spectral illumination of moonshine'

Heart of Darkness, p. 30

a sentence which reminds one of Virginia Woolf's description of life as

'a luminous halo, a semi-transparent envelope surrounding us from the beginning of consciousness to the end'

Forster is different but, like Conrad or Virginia Woolf, he treats 'story' in a cavalier fashion, 'throwing away' climaxes that Jane Austen or Dickens or George Eliot would have led up to carefully and taken trouble to make plausible; and the reason, I think, is that (though in many respects a fairly conventional novelist) he sees life as more basically wayward than, say, Dickens does and has fewer certainties. Dickens, for all his pleasure in idiosyncrasy and unexpectedness and his use of coincidence as hinges for his plots, hasn't much doubt that the world is there for men to control and subdue and that moral judgements are controlled by some sort of rationality. But Forster, like Lawrence, seems all the time to invoke some sort of 'passion', some new dimension in human potentiality, which is more or less self-justifying (you could say the same of Emily Brontë in the value she gives to the relationship between Catherine and Heathcliff).

The 'modernist' writers with whom we have ended this course seem to me to stand in a relationship to the nineteenth-century novelists which is fruitfully comparable with the relationship of the Romantic poets to the eighteenth-century Augustans. It's the *relationship* that's comparable, not of course the ideas or achievements of the individual writers, and I'm not suggesting that Joyce, say, is at all like Wordsworth. But just as Romanticism represents a breakthrough in human consciousness which also involves a loss, so—it seems to me—do the 'modernists' with their sense of a new complexity and at the same time of a new potential in human creativity. The loss is essentially, I think, a loss of a sense of 'belonging' and it is intricately bound up with the gains because no one, after all, wants to 'belong' to a society which he no longer feels helps him to live fully and creatively. Just as the Romantics *had to* break with the essentially 'aristocratic' values of Augustan literature (but in doing so tended to lose that rich apprehension of the 'established' elements of social living which served the Augustans), so were the 'modernists' impelled to break with the dominant values and perceptions of the 'establishment' of nineteenth-century Europe. But it is one thing to 'break with' established perceptions and values and another to find new and more valid means of coping with human existence. It's not hard to see in a general way why Virginia Woolf wanted to abandon 'story' as too rigid and contrived a mode for the expression of the flux of experience and the passage of time: it's less easy to assess confidently the gains and losses involved in her attempts to write novels at once more or less 'integrated' than those of her predecessors. The whole question of 'disintegration' at the turn of the century is one that has to be seen, I'd suggest, within a very large context of artistic change and experiment—not confined to the novel—in which illusion and advance, liberation and emptiness are unusually

24

hard to distinguish. The value of a glance at the virtual disappearance of 'story' from some of the most interesting novels of the early twentieth-century seems to me to lie in the opportunity it gives us to recognise how basic 'story' (in different guises) was to the nineteenth-century novelists and to pose the question: what need did it satisfy and why did it cease to satisfy that need?

I can't help feeling that this whole question—which is, incidentally, linked to the problem of how 'determinist' one's view of life is—is bound up, like so much in life, with questions of power. The reason Sir Thomas Bertram has such a confident, cut-and-dried view of life is at bottom that he is confident that he has the power to impose that view on his world. When he finds he has slipped up pretty badly in his daughter's education, he still has the power to 'deal with' the situation and, though his *amour-propre* and the happiness of those around him have received a serious jolt by the end of the novel, I don't think any reader feels that his (or Jane Austen's) way of looking at the world has taken a fatal blow. The blow suffered by the Bulstrodes in *Middlemarch* is a more desperate one; but even so it's absorbed, however painfully, within the fabric of the Middlemarch world. Middlemarch society is powerful enough (which means in practice the people with power in Middlemarch are sufficiently well entrenched) to 'deal with' the Bulstrodes. The shock-absorbers work. But you don't feel at the end of Hardy's novel that anyone has managed to 'deal with' Jude. What *he* stands for is unresolved: his death ends nothing. The people with power in his world have resisted his aspirations for the time being and seem to have humbled him and Sue but his cry echoes on reverberating *outside* his novel as nothing reverberates outside Mansfield Park or Middlemarch but as the sentence 'Mistah Kurtz—he dead' reverberates outside *Heart of Darkness* (for I don't think T. S. Eliot's taking up of the phrase is pure chance). I agree with Cicely Havely that the 'Victorian' aspects of Conrad's story, though they're there all right, aren't in the end the most important things about it.

Again, what's behind (or perhaps more accurately, embodied in) Hardy and Conrad, is a situation in which power is changing. One sort of power is threatened, another threatens, undermining and disintegrating established actions and attitudes, even though the new pattern is itself largely unrealised, undefined even.

I feel like stressing this point not in order to try to impose a closer relationship between 'literature' on the one hand and 'society' on the other than actually exists, but because it seems to me important to recognise that all human activity is interconnected. The energy that expresses itself in social organisation and the energy that expresses itself in art may be channelled in different ways but they are also the same energy. The tensions within a novel and the tensions within a society are in obvious ways distinguishable but in deeper ways closely related and even the same, for what changes the world is the exercise of power by actual people (including novelists) moved by actual necessities in actual situations. A story is a construction of incidents, motives and actions given certain relationships which the audience as well as the teller recognise as valid and significant. The relationships involved are neither eternal nor casual but have their own sort of logic which is inevitably linked with the life-experience and history of those who tell and those who receive the story.

Arnold Kettle has computed the balance of gain and loss involved in being a 'modernist' writer very convincingly, I think, But I would like to add a rider.

It is that one is sometimes tempted to feel sorry for 'modernist' writers, for suffering from the sense of 'not belonging' and for being forced by circumstances to write in a difficult and unpopular manner; but it is doubtful if they really need one's pity. What is striking about writers like Joyce and Lawrence, to my mind, is their extraordinary confidence in the powers of art, indeed their extraordinary confidence in themselves generally. This confidence went with a profound pessimism about society; nevertheless, a confidence it was. Far from being bewildered and melancholy, these 'modernist' writers were spokesmen of joy and energy, rudely bursting in upon the hushed reveries of the *fin-de-siècle*. Much of the writing of both Joyce and of Lawrence is a passionate paean of joy and faith in life. And not only that, they attempted and accomplished hugely ambitious projects. Nor was this confidence in art a sterile ivory-tower aestheticism. On the contrary, it represented, amongst other things, a victory for social egalitarianism. It is a striking fact that H. G. Wells and Arnold Bennett, though the one was of working-class and the other of lower-middle-class origin, were incapable of writing about working-class or lower-middle-class characters with any freedom or unselfconsciousness. They are always either harping on the social humiliations suffered by their working-class heroes, or facetiously glorifying the 'little man' and the 'wonderfulness' of suburban or small-town life, in an insincere and patronising manner. And there was good reason for this. For the conventions and assumptions of nineteenth-century fiction, those which I was attempting to analyse earlier in this Unit, were, through and through, upper-middle-class ones. The very prose-style of fiction and of literary journalism was, for good or ill, redolent of upper-middle-class and social attitudes.

Thus it was almost a measure of their genius that for Joyce and Lawrence this class problem was no longer a problem—that it dissolved at their touch, and they were able to write about working-class and lower-middle-class characters without these defensive postures. It was also a measure of, or at least was closely bound up with, their modernity and technical innovation. The very device of 'interior monologue', you might say, favours a freedom from class inhibition. Had Virginia Woolf systematically presented Miss Kilman through 'interior monologue' she would have been compelled to treat her with more sympathy; and Joyce's treatment of Bloom, in its sympathetic objectivity, is worlds away from Bennett and Wells and their patronising glorification of the 'little man'. Similarly, the directness and (in a good sense) 'man-to-man' quality of Lawrence's prose is, even by itself, a pledge and symbol of his having cut through class entanglements.

2.8   Imitative Form

Certainly, if a novelist does free himself from 'scaffolding' in the way we have described, a vast new range of possibilities opens up to him. One of these is *imitative form*—as practised by Joyce, Virginia Woolf and others. By imitative form I mean making the form of your writing imitate or 'enact' what is being said. Poetry has always used imitative form to a greater or lesser extent. (Put 'onomatopoeia' out of your head, if it was ever in it, as this refers to something rather trivial. What I am speaking of is subtler and more pervasive—for instance, the way that when Milton writes 'Illimitable Ocean without bound', the mere symmetry and logic of placing 'Illimitable' on one side of 'Ocean' and its exact synonym 'without bound' on the other strongly reinforce the idea of infinite and shoreless ocean.) In prose, however, imitative form has played a smaller part, and it would be hard to think of, say, George Eliot or Jane

Austen making much use of it: it would have cut across the conventions of their writing. Thus it is a real break with nineteenth-century fiction when, in Joyce, it suddenly begins to play a large and significant role. Joyce is a great master of imitative form. One has only to think of *Portrait of the Artist*, where, as Graham Martin points out in Unit 31, the sentence-structure grows progressively more elaborate as the hero grows older and learns to relate his experiences together in more complex ways. This device is a simple one, though a stroke of genius, and there are more elaborate kinds of imitation going on in the prose and structure of the book. However, anything he achieves here is outshadowed by what he does in *Ulysses*. It would be hard to imagine a more intensely vivid and imitatively expressive sentence than that one I quoted earlier from the 'Hades' section: 'The felly harshed against the curbstone: stopped.' A whole physical event has been captured by these few words. Clearly, something has happened to fiction when it can contain sentences such as this. A nineteenth-century novelist could not have written that sudden 'stopped', for he thinks of himself, all the time, as *conversing* with the reader, and this is not the prose of converse. He would have had to write, more weakly and conventionally, '*and the carriage* stopped'.

Here is another, rather similar, example of imitative form, used again for purposes of description:

Clay, brown, damp, began to be seen in the hole. It rose. Nearly over. A mound of damp clods rose more, rose, and the gravediggers rested their spades.

You might like to try picking out others of this type.

This, however, is only one of many kinds of imitative form in the 'Hades' section. Imitation is, for instance, a very important aspect of 'interior monologue', as Joyce practises it. One recognises Bloom instantly from the very syntax of his sentences—those choppy, staccato, elliptical sentences and half-sentences, often beginning with a verb. The syntax exactly catches his turn of mind, a busy, inquisitive, grasshopper mind, intelligent but totally directionless; the mind of an extrovert, who feels deeply but does not brood on his feelings, one moment mourning his father and his little son Rudy, the next moment inventing safety devices for coffins.

There are many other kinds of imitative form in Joyce, and indeed he is the supreme master of it in prose fiction. But it plays a considerable part in Virginia Woolf also, and you might find it a worth-while exercise to look at a page or two of *Mrs Dalloway* and spot and analyse the examples you find there. Look especially, for this purpose, at her prose *rhythm*, always wonderfully expressive, and often imitative in some fairly definable way (though of course there is no sharp dividing line between what is 'imitative' and what is simply 'expressive')

2.9   The Life of the Senses

I turn now to another new horizon, of a quite different kind, disclosed to the twentieth-century novelist. Joyce and Lawrence, as I need hardly say, were exceedingly unlike as men and as writers: the one so overridingly concerned with art, working a very rich vein of human material but from a standpoint of rigorous and aloof detachment; the other on such apparently easy terms with his human material, writing spontaneously and freely in the way that

one might talk. You might even think of them, as writers, as being exactly opposite types. Nevertheless, if you compare Joyce's 'The Dead' with Lawrence's 'The Fox', you may notice an interesting likeness; and it is one that—just because they are, temperamentally, so opposed—tends to suggest that there was such a thing as a 'modernist' movement in fiction. You might like to ask yourself what likeness I have in mind.

Discussion

I am thinking of the way in which, all through the New Year's Eve dance at the Miss Morkan's in 'The Dead', Gabriel Conroy keeps thinking of the snow outside the windows. With half his mind, he longs to be out in it, to feel its freshness and see its gleaming cleanness. It seems to have a message for him, to be a criticism of him and of the complacent second-rateness of the role he is playing that night and in life generally. And, as we find, it has indeed a message for him, a more far-reaching one even than that. But I won't repeat Graham Martin's analysis of this rich and complex story. What I am concerned with here is the likeness to March and her fox in the opening pages of Lawrence's *novella*. The fox scratches at the back of March's consciousness in the same irrational way as the snow in Joyce's story, as though it carried a message for her.

. . . whenever she fell into her half-musing, when she was half rapt and half intelligently aware of what passed under her vision, then it was the fox which somehow dominated her unconsciousness, possessed the blank half of her musing. And so it was for weeks and months.

In both cases, the experience belongs to the shadowed and subconscious part of the mind; and it is, in its way, a physical feeling—'It was as if she [March] could smell him'. In both stories physical instinct, a mood of the body, is telling the character something that is at odds with his rational account of things—something that, when it emerges in his conscious mind, drastically alters his idea of himself and transforms his existence.

Of course, Joyce and Lawrence were not the first to describe such a process. There is something not too dissimilar, for instance, in Tolstoy's account of Anna's railway journey in Part I, Chapter 29 of *Anna Karenina* (where the cold and snow play a part faintly reminiscent of their role in 'The Dead'). What is significant is that Joyce and Lawrence make it the very subject of their story. I would hazard that they were the first to do so. And it places them squarely in one of the main movements on European thought in their period. One of the leading notions in the arts, but also in psychology and other human sciences in the early twentieth-century, was that physical and instinctual experience conveyed truth, and a kind of truth that cut across the rational structures of ordinary moral and social thinking. I have put it in as broad and general a way as I could, and you may say it is too foggy a generalisation to be any use. Still I will stick by it for a moment and remind you of the trend I have in mind: Freudian psychology; the new anthropology, which dug down to the primitive roots of religion; the philosophies of Nietzsche and Bergson, with their appeal to instinct; music like Debussy's, which deserted the rational structures of sonata-form for something nearer the immediacy of sense-experience; poetry like T. S. Eliot's, which shuns 'ideas', in the ordinary cause of that word, and explores a 'feeling for syllable and rhythm, penetrating far below the conscious levels of thought and feeling'. I am not at all suggesting that Joyce and

Lawrence were doing the same thing as Freud or Debussy or Eliot (and in fact both Lawrence and Joyce were hostile to Freud, though certainly influenced by him too). The point I want to make, rather, is that this idea of a 'truth' in instinctual and physical experience was so pervasive that an arch-rationalist like Freud was as much committed to it as a visionary like Nietzsche. This is an unusual state of affairs, for normally rationalists and visionaries are natural enemies; and it suggests that what we have here is a definite historical event. Nineteenth-century society had, over the years, developed problems and tensions to which there was no solution in the accepted 'laws' of psychology and ethics—those 'laws' which nineteenth-century novelists were so expert in illustrating. The dilemma grew to a crisis, and the solution was felt to lie in that neglected area, the life of the senses. Thus, in constructing these stories of theirs, as they did, round a persistent, nagging intuition from the 'life of the senses', Joyce and Lawrence were in the central current of a larger intellectual movement. The likeness between 'The Dead' and 'The Fox' is not accidental.

2.10   D. H. Lawrence and Thomas Hardy

I have been trying to argue that it is not just a matter of date when we speak of Joyce, Virginia Woolf and D. H. Lawrence as belonging to the 'modernist' movement in fiction, and that they had some real community of purpose. Nevertheless this is a matter of hindsight, and you must not assume that Lawrence, say, felt any affinity with his contemporaries, or they with him. On the contrary, Lawrence thought of novelists like Joyce and Proust as utterly sterile and only fit for the operating-table. Here is what he said about them in an essay 'Surgery for the Novel—or a Bomb':

Is Ulysses in his cradle? Oh, dear! What a grey face! And *Pointed Roofs*,[1] are they a gay little toy for nice little girls? And M. Proust? Alas! You can hear the death-rattle in their throats. They can hear it themselves. They are listening to it with acute interest, trying to discover whether the intervals are minor thirds or major fourths. Which is rather infantile, really.

So there you have the 'serious' novel, dying in a very long-drawn-out fourteen-volume death-agony, and absorbedly, childishly interested in the phenomenon. 'Did I feel a twinge in my little toes, or didn't I?' asks every character of Mr Joyce or of Miss Richardson or M. Proust. . . . It is self-consciousness picked into such fine bits that the bits are most of them invisible, and you have to go by smell. Through thousands and thousands of pages Mr Joyce and Miss Richardson tear themselves to pieces, strip their smallest emotions to the finest threads, till you feel you are sewed inside a wool mattress that is being slowly shaken up, and you are turning to wool along with the rest of the wooliness.

It's awful. And it's childish It really is childish, after a certain age, to be absorbedly self-conscious. . . . The people in the serious novels are so absorbedly concerned with themselves and what they feel and don't feel, and how they react to every mortal button; and their audience as frenziedly absorbed in the application of the author's discoveries to their own reactions: 'That's me! That's exactly it! I'm just finding myself in this book!'

---

[1] A novel by Dorothy Richardson, who was a pioneer of the 'stream-of-consciousness' novel. Her reputation had been rather overshadowed by Virginia Woolf's.

His contemporaries returned the compliment. Joyce was supremely uninterseted in Lawrence, as he was in Proust and Virginia Woolf. And Virginia Woolf found Lawrence wearisome and doctrinaire. So much for novelists as critics, you might say in disgust. And I don't mean to discuss the rights and wrongs of Lawrence's judgement on his contemporaries here. I am interested in it for the light it throws on Lawrence himself and his position in regard to his nineteenth-century predecessors.

In the same essay he asks if we are to think of the novel as being in its cradle, with its full adulthood still before it, or as being on its death-bed: 'Do we bounce with joy thinking of the wonderful novelistic days ahead? Or do we grimly shake our heads and hope the wicked creature will be spared a little longer?' His answer is, that if Joyce and Proust, etc. are representative, then the novel is on its death-bed. For the trouble with Joyce and the rest is that they are too self-preoccupied. What good does it do us to know about Bloom's day in such obsessive detail, he demands? All it can give us is the pleasure of *recognition*, of saying 'That's just like me!'

Lawrence, I think, regards Joyce and the rest not as producing anything valuably new, and as being merely the running-to-seed of nineteenth-century fiction. For even in the great nineteenth-century novelists much of the interest lies in mere *recognition* (if not exactly in Lawrence's sense). For instance, shall we say, in the pages of almost all the great Victorian novelists, you will find portraits of *hypocrites*—religious hypocrites, philanthropic hypocrites, artistic hypocrites—Bulstrode, Wopsle, Mme Stahl, etc. A nineteenth-century novelist would, I think, consider that to delineate, with exact social detail, a new but recognisable variety of the age-old species *the hypocrite* was sufficient and worthwhile for its own sake. For Lawrence, if I may so interpret him, this is no longer enough for the novel to be doing. The pleasure involved is too much the pleasure of mere recognition—it is just society looking at its own likeness in a mirror. He believes the novel has a more strenuous function. He wants a novel which could survive the blowing-up of society as at present constituted and thus different from the kind of novel which merely mirrors society.

Supposing a bomb were put under the whole scheme of things, what would we be after? What feelings do we want to carry through into the next epoch? What feelings will carry us through? What is the underlying impulse in us that will provide the motive power for a new state of things, when this democratic-industrial-lovey-dovey-darling-take-me-to-mamma state of things is bust?

What next? That's what interests me. 'What now' is no fun any more.

To some extent I have been putting words into Lawrence's mouth, as regards the nineteenth-century novel, so it is instructive to see him discussing a Victorian novelist himself, as he does in his 'Study of Thomas Hardy'. This is a very strange, powerful, rambling (or apparently rambling) work, which deals not just with Hardy but everything else under the sun. It is one of the central statements of Lawrence's philosophy, and I can't deal with it in general here, nor will I even attempt to assess its validity as a critique of Hardy. The point I want to make here is more specific. It is that for Lawrence the ultimate purpose of life was the creation of unique, unrepeatable individuals, and why Hardy inspired and interested him so peculiarly was because, of all Victorian novels, Hardy's seemed most in sympathy with this theory. In Hardy, the interest is certainly not merely that of recognising ourselves or recognising truths already known to us.

It is urged against Thomas Hardy's characters that they do unreasonable things—quite, quite unreasonable things. They are always off unexpectedly, and doing something that nobody would do. That is quite true, and the charge is amusing. These people of Wessex are always bursting suddenly out of bud and taking a wild flight into flower, always shooting suddenly out of a tight convention, a tight, hidebound cabbage state into something quite madly personal.

Thus, in singling out Hardy for praise, Lawrence is making a general critique of the nineteenth-century novel. Only there was a snag. Hardy, so thought Lawrence, did not understand his own purposes sufficiently and sometimes was untrue to his own instincts. In fact, he made a muddle of his novels. And so Lawrence, with cheerful effrontery, proceeds to rewrite them for us in the way they should really have been written. He tells us, for instance, that Hardy really admired the natural human 'aristocrats'—those who have the courage to believe in themselves and be damned to public opinion—more than he allows himself to admit. Arabella, in *Jude the Obscure*, was 'under all her disguise of pig-fat and false hair, and vulgar speech, in character somewhat an aristocrat'. Hardy has played her false.

He insists that she is a pig-killer's daughter; he insists that she drag Jude into pig-killing; he lays stress on her false tail of hair. That is not the point at all. This is only Hardy's bad art. He himself, as an artist, manages in the whole picture of Arabella almost to make insignificant in her these pig-sticking, false-hair crudities. But he must have his personal revenge on her for her coarseness, which offends him. . . . The pig-sticking and so forth are not so important in the real picture. As for the false tail of hair, few women would have dared to have been so open and natural about it.

Lawrence's is an odd, and impudent, and absurdly high-handed way of treating another artists's works; all the same, on reflection, there's something in it. I think one *is* bothered by that business of Arabella's false hair. It seems too naïve, too childish, a fictional device to be offered seriously as a major stage in Jude's disillusionment And so Lawrence's explanation begins to carry a certain weight.

Lawrence justifies his high-handed approach on the grounds that a novelist has a particular temptation to be untrue to his instincts. A novelist, much more than a lyric poet or a writer of moral essays, has to have a complete theory of the universe—for it is impossible to describe the world without some framework of theory. And if he happens to have no natural talent for metaphysics he may easily find himself squaring the world to fit a crude theory. This happened with Hardy, Lawrence thinks, as it did with Tolstoy (see Unit 26, p. 47), and thus Hardy is often untrue to his own best instincts.

But often, too, he is faithful to them and expresses them beyond all shadow of misunderstanding. And whatever you may think of Lawrence's general approach to Hardy—and I would quarrel with a good deal of it myself—his tribute to what he admires in Hardy is extremely fine.

This is a constant revelation in Hardy's novels: that there exists a great background, vital and vivid, which matters more than the people who move upon it. . . . The little fold of law and order, the little walled city within which man has to defend himself from the waste enormity of nature, becomes always too small, and the pioneers venturing out with the code of the walled city upon them, die in the bonds of that code, free and yet unfree, preaching the walled city and looking to the waste.

This is the wonder of Hardy's novels, and gives them their beauty. The vast, unexplored morality of life itself, what we call the immorality of nature, surrounds us in its eternal incomprehensibility, and in its midst goes on the little human morality play, with its queer frame of morality and its mechanized movement; seriously, portentously, till some one of the protagonists chances to look out of the charmed circle, weary of the stage, to look into the wilderness raging round.

Lawrence compares this quality, which for him is the strong and true quality in Hardy, to that of Sophocles and Shakespeare But his sentence about the protagonist who 'chances to look out of the charmed circle, weary of the stage, to look into the wilderness raging round' reminds me of someone else too—and that is Conrad's Marlow in *Heart of Darkness* It is surely a very apt description of Conrad's purposes in *Heart of Darkness*. And by making this the explicit subject of his story, I would suggest, Conrad is exemplifying, as in his own way Lawrence himself exemplifies, one of the characteristic preoccupations of 'modernist' fiction.

2.11   Virginia Woolf and Joyce

I turn now to another interesting literary relationship, that between Virginia Woolf and Joyce. Arnold Kettle has already discussed Virginia Woolf's essays 'Modern Fiction' and 'Mr Bennett and Mrs Brown', but I will remind you here of their drift. She accuses the Edwardian novel, the novel of Wells, Arnold Bennett and Galsworthy, of being too materialistic. When Bennett, in his novel *Hilda Lessways*, ought to be telling us about his heroine, and seizing her essential identity, he insists instead, she says, on telling us about the sort of house she sees from her window and the sort of house she lives in: '. . . we cannot hear her mother's voice, or Hilda's voice; we can only hear Mr Bennett's voice telling us facts about rents, and freeholds and copyholds and fines'. With all his powers of observation, which are marvellous, with all his sympathy and humanity, which are great, Bennett has never looked directly at human nature. Virginia Woolf takes as her example of human nature an elderly woman with whom she once shared a railway carriage from Richmond to Waterloo, and about whom—though they never spoke—she instantly felt a duty and compulsion to 'realize her character' and 'steep herself in her atmosphere'. There she sits, this old lady whom we will call Mrs Brown, says Virginia Woolf, 'and not one of the Edwardian writers have so much as looked at her'. She returns to the theme in 'Modern Fiction': 'It is because they [Wells, Bennett and Galsworthy] are concerned not with the spirit but with the body that they have disappointed us, and left us with the feeling that the sooner English fiction turns its back upon them as politely as may be, and marches, if only into the desert, the better for its soul.'

She regards Joyce as one of those who have 'marched into the desert'. In 1919 when she had read only a fragment of *Ulysses*, she paid high tribute to Joyce.

In contrast with those whom we have called materialists, Mr Joyce is spiritual; he is concerned at all costs to reveal the flickerings of that innermost flame which flashes its messages through the brain, and in order to preserve it he disregards with complete courage whatever seems to him adventitious, whether it be probability, or coherence, or any other of those signposts which for generations have served to support the imagination of a reader when called upon to imagine what he can neither touch nor see. The scene in the cemetery, for instance, with its brilliancy, its sordidity, its incoherence, its sudden lightning flashes of significance, does undoubtedly come so close to the quick of the mind that, on first reading at any rate, it is difficult not to acclaim a masterpiece.

It was a very perceptive, if also—with its exclusive stress on inwardness and 'the quick of life'—a very Woolfian view of Joyce. She qualified her praise, however, by asking why, after all, work of such originality failed to measure up to true masterpieces like those of Conrad and Hardy.

It fails because of the comparative poverty of the writer's mind, we might say simply and have done with it. But it is possible to press a little further and wonder whether we may not refer our sense of being in a bright yet narrow room, confined and shut in, rather than enlarged and set free, to some limitation imposed by the method as well as by the mind. Is it the method that inhibits the creative power? Is it due to the method that we feel neither jovial nor magnanimous, but centred in a self which, in spite of its tremor of susceptibility, never embraces or creates what is outside itself and beyond? Does the emphasis laid, perhaps didactically, upon indecency, contribute to the effect of something angular and isolated?

She finds Joyce egocentric; and in that she echoes D. H. Lawrence (see p. 29). She also finds his method cramping and confining; or perhaps it is that, for her, there is simply *too much* method in his writing. And she dislikes his indecency and literary 'bad manners', his rough handling of the reader. Later, she seems to have hardened against Joyce, and it was the indecency which most weighted with her. 'Mr Joyce's indecency in *Ulysses*', she says in 'Mr Bennett and Mrs Brown', 'seems to me the conscious and calculated indecency of a desperate man who feels that in order to breathe he must break the windows. At moments, when the window is broken, he is magnificent. But what a waste of energy!' England, she says, is trembling on the verge of a great age in its literature (this was in 1924) but has not yet entered it: for the moment one must not expect a complete and satisfactory presentment of 'Mrs Brown' —that is to say, of eternal human nature—and must be tolerant of 'the spasmodic, the obscure, the fragmentary, the failure'.

Considering the gross indifference of Joyce and Lawrence to their fellows in the 'modernist' movement, Virginia Woolf's response to Joyce does her credit. And, as I have suggested earlier, she was deeply influenced by him, probably more than she realised. All the same, I find it striking that she should have felt so much resistance to Joyce—who, you might feel, fulfilled her demands from the novel with extraordinary completeness. Partly, no doubt, it was a matter of temperament and upbringing: for, for all her emancipation, there always remained something 'ladylike', in a slightly cramping way, about Virginia Woolf. But what was also involved, I think, was a misreading of literary history. Virginia Woolf regarded Bennett and Wells and Galsworthy as in the mainstream of the realist tradition, whereas they were a backwater of it. The main current of the 'realist' and 'naturalist' tradition, the heroic tradition of Balzac, Flaubert and Zola, ran through Joyce. He was their true inheritor, and in his going beyond them something curious took place. By taking to extremes the 'materialism' of the realist novel—its solidity and scientific matter-of-factness and mass of petty and often squalid detail—he dematerialised and spiritualised it. In the 'Hades' extract from *Ulysses* there is plenty of stress on externals. Joyce's method is not so far off the one caricatured by Virginia Woolf in 'Mr Bennett and Mrs Brown':

Begin by saying that her father kept a shop in Harrogate. Ascertain the rent. Ascertain the wages of shop assistants in the year 1878. Discover what her mother died of. Describe cancer. Describe calico. Describe . . .

Joyce does not merely begin by saying such things, he goes on saying them. Even during this funeral-scene we get to know quite a little about Bloom's business methods, and opera in Ireland, and Dublin topography, let alone about the small change of Bloom's mind, the bad puns, *Tit-Bits* information, discomfort about a cake of soap and reminders to himself to change his wife's library book. Yet 'life', indisputably, does *not* escape, it does not refuse to inhabit this mansion, and is happy to live in these petty 'external' details. And through them we perceive things as inward and profound as we could wish for: virtue in action, racial suffering, and an epic vision of the grave.

2.12   What the Novel Can Do

Let us come back, finally, to the claims made for the art of fiction by these writers and ask what their claims have in common, if anything, and how they differ from the claims of earlier novelists. You have already read those famous literary *credos* of Joyce, Lawrence and Virginia Woolf, but I will quote them again.

Here are Joyce's:

By an epiphany he meant a sudden spiritual manifestation, whether in vulgarity of speech or of gesture or in a memorable phrase of the mind itself. He believed that it was for the man of letters to record these epiphanies with extreme care, seeing that they themselves are the most delicate and evanescent of moments.

The artist, like the God of creation, remains within or behind or beyond or above his handiwork, invisible, refined out of existence, indifferent, paring his fingernails.

I go to encounter for the millionth time the reality of experience and to forge in the smithy of my soul the uncreated conscience of my race.

Here is Lawrence's:

It is the way our sympathy flows and recoils that really determines our lives. And here lies the vast importance of the novel, properly handled. It can inform and lead into new places the flow of our sympathetic consciousness, and it can lead our sympathy away in recoil from things gone dead.

And here is Virginia Woolf's:

Examine for a moment an ordinary mind on an ordinary day. The mind receives a myriad impressions—trivial, fantastic, evanescent, or engraved with the sharpness of steel. From all sides they come, an incessant shower of innumerable atoms; and as they fall, as they shape themselves into the life of Monday or Tuesday, the accent falls differently from of old; the moment of importance came not here but there; so that, if a writer were a free man and not a slave, if he could write what he chose, not what he must, if he could base his work upon his own feeling and not upon convention, there would be no plot, no comedy, no tragedy, no love interest or catastrophe in the accepted style, and perhaps not a single button sewn on as the Bond Street tailors would have it. Life is not a series of gig lamps symmetrically arranged; life is a luminous halo, a semi-transparent envelope surrounding us from the beginning of consciousness to the end. Is it not the task of the novelist to convey this varying, this unknown and uncircumscribed spirit, whatever aberration or complexity it may display, with as little of the alien and external as possible?

These *credos* or programmes are very different, and I will not repeat the work of earlier units by analysing them. But, as well as very different, are they alike in any way—any way that is as interesting as their difference?

Well, I would suggest one likeness: all three writers make very high claims indeed for fiction. For Lawrence, the novel is a kind of Moses, leading the reader out of the captivity of the habitual into a new Promised Land. (Significantly it is the novel, not the novelist, that he pictures acting as Moses—Lawrence is not promoting a Romantic personality-cult.) For Joyce, the novelist is a wonder-worker, a rival to God and a shower-forth of eternal realities; his 'epiphanies', though seized in a fleeting moment, reveal permanent forms and patterns. (For him the stress is on the novelist, and he is, to that extent, more in the Romantic tradition.) Lastly there is Virginia Woolf, for whom the novelist is a superfine recording instrument or sensitised plate. Her position is closer to pure aestheticism. Art for life's sake, as she defines it, is not so very far from art for art's sake, and her credo has a little of the accent of that most famous credo of aestheticism, Pater's words in *The Renaissance*:

Analysis . . . assures us that those impressions of the individual mind to which, for each one of us, experience dwindles down, are in perpetual flight; that each of them is limited by time, and that as time is infinitely divisible, each of them is infinitely divisible also; all that is actual in it being a single moment, gone while we try to apprehend it, of which it may ever be more truly said that it has ceased to be than it is. To such a tremulous wisp constantly reforming itself on the stream, to a single sharp impression, with a sense in it, a relic more or less fleeting, of such moments gone by, what is real in our life fines itself down. It is with this movement, with the passage and dissolution of impressions, images, sensation, that analysis leaves off—that continual vanishing away, that strange, perpetual, weaving and unweaving of ourselves.

. . . Every moment some form grows perfect in hand or face; some tone on the hills or the sea is choicer than the rest; some mood of passion or insight or intellectual excitement is irresistibly real and attractive for us—for that moment only. Not the fruit of experience, but experience itself, is the end.

The claim made for fiction by Virginia Woolf is perhaps not quite so high as that made by Lawrence and Joyce. Nevertheless it is a high claim too: fiction is to capture nothing less than (and nothing apart from) 'life' itself—with the implication that no one but a writer or artist could achieve such a feat.

In making these high claims for fiction, higher perhaps than any made for it before, these three novelists of ours are at one with modernist artists in general. The writers and painters and poets of their period have extraordinary confidence in the powers of art, and by virtue of it they despise politicians and feel no kind of inferiority to scientists (Lawrence called the novel 'a great discovery: far greater than Galileo's telescope or somebody else's wireless'). What this goes with, however, and indeed it is another way of putting it, is a profound pessimism about society. We see it in Joyce, who spoke of 'that hemiplegia or paralysis which many consider a city', and again in Lawrence, who had apocalyptic feelings of doom about English society. With Virginia Woolf the pessimism is a little more personal but still strong: it is a despair of there being more than a few unpredictable moments of pattern and meaningfulness in the random flux of events and jostling of isolated souls. For all three writers the confidence and the pessimism go hand in hand and the resulting outlook is rather different from that of nineteenth-century novelists. The novel for them is to be a kind of ark riding out the flood.[1]

[1] I said earlier (page 20) that one of the characteristic ambitions of modernist novelists was to capture the whole of something, or to get everything in. My metaphor of the ark has a certain aptness to this too.

2.13   APPENDIX 1

Which Changes First: the Novel or Reality?

NICK FURBANK: In this Unit I have tried to analyse twentieth-century developments in fiction 'from inside'—that is to say from what I imagine to have been
the point of view of a writer coming to maturity in the early years of the
century. Of course, I might also have tried to see the same things from the
outside—more purely historically, that is to say. Many critics would argue
that why Joyce, Lawrence and Virginia Woolf felt the need to create new forms
of fiction was because 'reality' or human nature had changed, and thus new
forms were required to express it. There is a good deal to be said for this view,
but on balance I am, personally, inclined to attribute less influence to the
'spirit of the age' and more to the artist himself and the internal necessities of
his art. For one thing, the idea of 'everything' changing at one moment of
time seems to make too much of a straight line, to much of a concrete motorway,
of history. And for another, the theory tends to diminish the active and dynamic
role of artists. After all, artists don't merely express the reality about them,
they also change it; they are active forces in history, and the world can never
be the same once they have seen it with new eyes.

However, I have an important witness, Virginia Woolf herself, against me. In
'Mr Bennett and Mrs Brown' she says:

. . . in or about December 1910, human character changed.

I am not saying that one went out, as one might into a garden, and there saw
that a rose had flowered, or that a hen had laid an egg. The change was not
sudden and definite like that. But a change there was, nevertheless; and, since
one must be arbitrary, let us date it about the year 1910. . . . All human
relations have shifted—those between masters and servants, husbands and
wives, parents and children. And when human relations change there is at
the same time a change in religion, conduct, politics and literature.

She, if anyone, has a right to be listened to in this Course. And as Arnold Kettle
differs from me a little on this subject, and holds views nearer to Virginia
Woolf's, I would like him to bring this Unit to a conclusion.

ARNOLD KETTLE: I am one of those who would be inclined to give more
weight to the changes in 'reality' to which Nick Furbank refers. I should stress,
though, before going any further, that I don't want to try to 'polarise' a
disagreement which is certainly not an absolute one and may be more obvious
in a theoretical discussion of principles than in the actual practice of discussing
and evaluating particular books and the ideas connected with them.

The whole problem, of course, involves the general question of the relationship
of literature to socio-historical developments, or, as it's raised in Unit 1 and
elsewhere in the Course, the relationship of novels to their context, and if
you have time you might re-read Unit 1, Section 6, in which I first touched
on the general problem. As a matter of fact I think it can be misleading even
to call the problem 'the relationship of literature to society or context' because
in a *general* discussion of that question Nick Furbank and I would almost
certainly be in substantial agreement. We'd agree that novels come out of a
particular social context and also that 'artists don't merely express the reality

about them, they also change it'. In other words, that the relationship is a two-way one and not a matter of mere 'reflection' of a separate, outside reality by the artist. So I don't want to stress the differences in our emphasis However, if I were going to state my own general position on these matters I'd want to say something like the following: that we are all of us—novelists, the people in their novels, and readers (that's to say you and I)—characters in history and have no being or existence except as such. And this leads me to be very suspicious of any tendency to play down 'context' in discussing literature. For I'd risk the generalisation that for most of us (as far as literary criticism goes) the greater danger is to be insufficiently aware of ourselves as characters in history than insufficiently 'blank' or 'open' in our responses. It seems to me that most of our more 'instinctive' judgements have elements of prejudice, complacency and egotism which can only be counteracted by a very persistent effort to see ourselves as what I've called 'characters in history' or, if you like, to see *ourselves*, as well as what we're reading, as objectively as possible

When I suggest that it's important to recognise that between 1816 (the year of *Mansfield Park*) and 1847 (the year of *Wuthering Heights*) something happened—or became more manifest—which made it possible for Emily Brontë to see reality in quite a different way from Jane Austen, I'm not implying that the changes involved were simple processes that can be summed up in a few glib sentences. Nor am I suggesting that the changes—social, psychological, conceptual—are somehow separate from and independent of the novels we've been reading and in some easy way 'explain' those novels. On the contrary, it's because *Wuthering Heights* is the book it is that we are aware of the nature of the changes that have taken place. A novel is a power.

There had been a 'breakthrough', which like almost all such changes, isn't simply and unequivocally an advance, though I think it is reasonable to argue that the human gain involved is, for some people and perhaps 'humanity' as a whole, real.

What precisely is the nature of the 'breakthrough' I'm talking about? To try to answer that question satisfactorily would involve us in a wide variety of questions—historical, philosophical, psychological (to say nothing of economic, technological or religious ones)—which obviously we can't begin to puzzle out here. If you happened to take the Age of Revolutions Course (A202) you'll have a good general idea of the sort of thing I have in mind.[1] And since there isn't much point in vague, unsubstantiated generalisations, perhaps the best way in practice of discussing this question of the relation of the nineteenth-century novel to its context is to take limited issues and talk about *them*. Nick Furbank's discussion of philanthropy (pp. 12–13 above) is a good example. Or it would be, I think, a profitable exercise to define and compare the meanings of the word 'love' in *Mansfield Park*, *Wuthering Heights* and *Jude the Obscure*. You would certainly find that any satisfactory definition of the differences between the love-feelings of (a) Fanny and Edmund, (b) Catherine and Heathcliff and (c) Sue and Jude would involve not only a comparison of the attitudes, language and values of the three authors but a sense of the changing social reality within which they operate and to which they contribute. When Jude lies dying he makes a desperate attempt to make sense of what has happened to his life.

'As for Sue and me when we were at our best, long ago—when our minds were clear and our love of truth fearless—the time was not ripe for us! Our ideas were fifty years too soon to be any good to us. And so the resistance they met

---

[1] Stimulating recent discussion of some of them is in Raymond Williams's *The Country and the City* (Chatto & Windus, 1973).

with brought reaction in her, and recklessness and ruin on me! . . . There— this, Mrs Edlin, is how I go on to myself continually, as I lie here. I must be boring you awfully.'

'Not at all, my dear boy I could hearken to 'ee all day . . .'

The very way Hardy relates this scene invites us to ask the question: is what Jude says true? It isn't just a question of Jude's explaining himself, expressing his own feelings, though of course that enters into it. Isn't the essential point the fact that we, the readers, have ourselves to assess the situation, ourselves decide whether Jude is at bottom a self-deceiver who has spent his life deluding himself, or whether what he says does actually correspond with reality? Is it the essential fact about his tragedy that the sort of relationship he and Sue were seeking was 'fifty years too soon'? And to answer *that* question don't we have to refer to something outside the novel, to the whole process of social development of the Victorian era—and afterwards? For part of the reason why we do, in my estimation, take Jude seriously and view Sue sympathetically, despite everything, is that subsequent history and our own experience have proved that the insights embedded in Hardy's novel are genuine insights into the human situation of both his and our time.

I agree, of course, with Nick Furbank that it is unrealistic and much too simple to imagine that 'everything' can change at a certain moment of time. Certainly Virginia Woolf didn't mean her placing of a change in human character at a certain date in 1910 to be taken too literally. Yet some sentences in that essay of hers about the need for a 'new' novel strike me as particularly illuminating. To illustrate her point about human change in the early twentieth century she wrote:

'In life one can see the change, if I may use a homely illustration, in the character of one's cook. The Victorian cook lived like a leviathan in the lower depths, formidable, silent, obscure, inscrutable; the Georgian cook is a creature of sunshine and fresh air; in and out of the drawing-room, now to borrow the *Daily Herald*, now to ask advice about a hat.'

Now this may be in some ways vulnerable as social history: one can recall cooks from Victorian novels who are not at all silent, obscure or inscrutable. Yet it's a good illustration of the point Virginia Woolf's making, because the changing position of servants and—equally—the altering attitudes of middle-class people towards servants, are just such significant indications as force people to see not just a particular 'social problem' but the whole world, and them-selves included, in different ways. One of the things about the passage I've just quoted is how socially 'dated' it already is within fifty years. Virginia Woolf feels she is pretty emancipated in her attitude to the cook and the *Daily Herald*. But by now the social context has so changed that her world seems almost as distant to us as the early Victorian household did to her.

One of the dangers, it would seem to me, of basing an approach to literature too much on 'the artist himself and the internal necessities of his art' (essential as these are) is that it can lead one to underplay the key importance of 'content' in the modification of 'form'. I think the work of E. M. Forster is a good example. If you approach him from a predominantly 'literary' standpoint you tend to emphasise the conservative aspect of his art. *Where Angels Fear to Tread* is then seen as not much different from a Victorian novel, in spite of a certain irrever-ence embodied in Forster's style. But if you concentrate more on the nature of the 'passion' which Forster sets up as the antithesis of the suburban com-placency centred on Sawston, then I think you're likely to be struck by the links between Forster and Lawrence rather than his affinities with, say, Jane Austen. The sense one gets from *Where Angels Fear to Tread* that the values of the Herritons are in some basic sense inimical to the values of creative living and that escape from Sawston involves a pretty drastic breaking through to an altogether different conception of value seems to me to put Forster—though obviously not an 'experimental' writer in the formal sense—definitely among the twentieth- rather than the nineteenth-century novelists.

I'd like at this point to risk a generalisation which you may disagree with or at least find vulnerable. (If you do you'll also query Nick Furbank's point developed on p. 7 which links closely with mine.) The most compelling conclusion I find myself drawing from the glance back at the nineteenth-century novel which our excursion into the twentieth has allowed us, is a conviction that the whole nature of the nineteenth-century novel depends on a sense of 'belonging' which all the nineteenth-century novelists seem to have in relation to the world they are writing about. I've argued elsewhere in the Course that this sense of 'belonging' changes in the course of the century and that the later novelists, at least in England, tend to withdraw from the sort of participation in social reality which a Dickens or a Balzac enjoys. But the contrasts between, say, Jane Austen and Dickens on the one hand and George Eliot and Henry James on the other are comparatively slight when you compare any of them with, say, Joyce or Virginia Woolf. Despite their differences among themselves in 'point of view', critical stance and other contrasts, *all* the nineteenth-century novelists seem to share certain pretty basic assumptions: that one thing leads with a relative certainty to another so that the relation between cause and effect and the whole business of the passage of time is fairly straightforward; that 'character' is discussable on the basis of how people behave; that it is possible for one person to understand another and even to describe him satisfactorily from the outside; that the boundary between sanity and madness is relatively clear. All these assumptions, I think, begin to be questioned in the early twentieth century, and basically because the novelists have no longer, in the same way, this sense of belonging. 'When I do not know any longer who are the "we" to whom I belong, I do not know any longer who "I" am either.'[1]

In some respects 'Which changes first: the novel or "reality"?' is a classic chicken-or-egg question which may seem to have no useful answer. But I'd argue that because novels are part of reality, contributing to it yet also dependent on it, one always must in the end give 'changing reality' a certain priority. I'm not so sure that the chicken-and-egg problem is meaningless anyway. It seems safe to assume that the first chicken came out of an egg: but that egg must have been laid by something not quite a chicken?

[1] The quotation is from *Crisis and Criticism* by Alick West (Lawrence & Wishart, 1937), at present out of print.

2.14   APPENDIX 2 (by Nuala O'Faolain)

Television and the Novel Course

University level broadcasting is new, and therefore contentious, and I'd like to discuss the particular question of television and the novel. But this is not an attempt to survey the broadcast element of the novel course. By their nature, the television and radio programmes were a passing experience for you.

It seems to me that there are overwhelmingly good reasons for using television and radio in arts courses generally. Broadcasting introduces teachers, experts, enthusiasts, to the isolated student. It brings places and performances to the home. It provides a common experience for a scattered body of students. More importantly, I believe that programmes often provide a non-inhibiting entry into new material for a student daunted by printed matter.

However, the novel is always a special case. The language of fiction is itself a distinctive medium, and a fiction has a perfectly self-sufficient life of its own. So, it is argued, other media are either irrelevant or damaging to the autonomy of the novel. It is perfectly possible to sharpen one's sense of what a novel is by opposing it to television and rejecting any relation between the two. Yet in this Course we have, though indirectly, related the two.

This is not because we think that reading a novel is an experience like watching television. A programme can never stand in for the crucially direct relationship between a novel and its reader. But, of course, there may be a phrase or an idea in an programme which helps to form that direct relationship, or helps to form the student's articulation of the relationship.

Also, a novel exists in multiple relations: with its author, its period, its interpreters, with literary history, with us. A student of the novel explores these on the basis of that primary relationship which he forms with the book when he reads it for itself. And television programmes can properly explore these too.

The sixteen television programmes of the Course are very diverse. Let me comment on some of them.

Programme 10, 'Words, Pictures and the Novel', and *programme* 6, 'The Victorian Reading Public' are surely non-controversial, since they're demonstrative and largely about the social history of literature. *Programme 1* about 'Improvement' in *Mansfield Park*, and *programme 7* about the shock of Rome to Dorothea in *Middlemarch* are really not controversial either. The author of each programme proposed a suggestive but oblique perspective on to the novel. No one could suppose that the ambiguities of 'improvement' for Jane Austen or of history for George Eliot are central to reading *Mansfield Park* or *Middlemarch* with pleasure and understanding. But they are propositions appropriate to reading for study, when one goes back to novels in a deliberate and self-conscious way. Since both the programme ideas are rooted in the visual, and since they are not proposed as an authoritative explication, television is their natural medium.

A much more questionable use is made of landscape in *programme 2*, on Emily Brontë, and *programme 3*, 'Dickens and Great Expectations'. Obviously, locale was given so high an importance by these writers that it somewhere has a claim on the attention of the student. But two questions arise. When the film-maker selects a view of, say, the marshes near Gravesend, does his view intercept Dickens's? And, what is the status of biographical fact—the kitchen at Haworth, or the model for Satis House—when the centre of what's being studied is the fiction?

The first of these questions is almost rhetorical. A feature film from a novel, made by a brilliant director and seen in the conditions of a cinema, might be able to blot out the private pictures we form in reading. Television is less impressive. But even television can deposit an image—of the Yorkshire moors or the Thames estuary—not authorised by *Wuthering Heights* or *Great Expectations*. These are the images that the purist feels are harmful to his sense of the novel. But how can they be more harmful than the memory of every moor or every river the reader has even seen? Do they not, in fact, direct the eye and the mind's eye away from the chaos of 'moor' and 'river', towards the world of the book? The same sort of directive impression is gained by physically visiting places; just as we narrow our concentration towards, say, Hardy, by visiting Dorchester, we narrow our concentration towards Pip's world by visiting the graveyard at Cooling.

The images we retain from the visit, or from viewing the film are not capable of being (or intended to be) authoritative in the way the whole book is, but they can pleasurably initiate attention to the book.

The only purely biographical programme is 'Tolstoy after *Anna Karenina*'. It doesn't raise the issue of 'what has the author's life got to do with his book'—because only the exceptionally reflective student will want to relate the last forty years of Tolstoy's life to *Anna Karenina*, and only the very ingenious will be able to.

One aspect of Zola—his feelings towards class—and one of Hardy—his feelings toward education—are used respectively by John Berger and Melvyn Bragg in their programmes on *Germinal* and *Jude the Obscure*.

Again, these programmes evade criticism. The comments of practising novelists on their distinguished predecessors are privileged; they tend to go through biography towards a general view of the 'creation' and 'craft' in fiction. The defect of this authority is that the student can't assume it himself, so these programmes are not exemplary in the way that programmes by critics are.

The biographical element in other programmes is more suspect. We don't need to see a portrait of Emily Brontë to know she existed. But I think that there is a stage, as we come to terms with novels, where biography is something we cling to. And not improperly. It is quite difficult to credit a fiction with the same kind of reality as our own experience, and knowing about the author's life helps the shift of trust.

Finally, Professor Kettle presented two programmes on television and the novel. They were especially concerned with turning attention back to the uniqueness of time, incident and character in the novel, through considering television dramatisation. They invited us to a consideration of the cultural position we inhabit. We are not pure of influences on our responses to nineteenth-century fiction. The dominant media of entertainment now are film and television, and this is probably more true the younger and the less educated one is. There is no way (except in the ways it wins for itself) that printed fiction can be separated at the surface of our impressions from all the other narratives we've received.

Radio and television are the first book-like media to have entered the home. They co-exist with books within an individual life. So the members of a university, above all, must recognise that a new area of discrimination is now open, and that one cannot dismiss the relationships between television and the novel as unworthy of serious exploration. To altogether ignore or resist the broadcast element of the novel course seems to me to imply either an excessively defensive view of the novel's autonomy, or an excessively innocent apprehension of the atmosphere of life now, the 'now' in which, perforce, we read the novels of the nineteenth-century.

A Final Word from the Course Team Chairman

We—the Course Team, that is—don't want to close the Course with a glib attempt to 'sum up' what we think you should have got out of it. We hope the Course has been more worthwhile than that sort of summary would imply. So if I mention, in closing, a few of the issues which we hope some of you may feel like returning to—and following up in the future—it's not to be taken as some pretentious form of moralising. One of the points that must have emerged from your reading of our novels is the sense that the relation between moral and story, between conclusion and experience, is generally a complex one, as complex as the way life itself operates.

Literary criticism isn't a technique, nor even, I think, what the educationalists refer to as a 'skill', though one wouldn't want to deny that some skills enter into it. If I say it's development of sensitivity, that sounds a bit pompous and might suggest that those of us who try our hand at it think we're a specially 'sensitive' brand of humanity. Heaven forbid. What I'm wanting to get at is an expression of my sense that studying literature involves in the reader both an openness to experience, a respect for what he's reading, and a desire to come to terms not only with it but with what nourishes or weakens it. This is what literary critics mean by 'evaluation', and it involves an extension of one's critical awareness—moral, historical and psychological as well as linguistic— centred around the selection of words which the writer has set before his readers. But no amount of critical theory can make possible the experience of being stirred by literature: only our lives can do that.

We hope you have enjoyed and profited from your reading of the individual novels. We hope you've found some of the 'general' and 'linking' material suggestive and helpful. And we hope you've acquired the confidence, during the year, to resist any ideas or judgements of members of the Course Team, if you have come to feel they are ill-based or in any way unconvincing. Above all we hope you have ended the Course with an increased pleasure in and respect for the nineteenth-century novel.

If this Course has been any good it's because of the sort of team-work and the sort of interaction between people (including students) the Open University makes possible. So when you think of the Course Team don't just think of those who put their names to the units or appear on television. There really is a team at work and it really is impossible to separate out one person's contribution from another's. You can continue this team-work by letting us have your criticism or suggestions about this Course and this will be helpful, not only in any revising of this particular Course but in the collective experience which will, in all sorts of complex ways, go into future Open University courses.

Acknowledgements

Grateful acknowledgement is made to the following sources for illustrations used on the cover of this unit:

Jane Austen: National Portrait Gallery; Balzac: Mansell Collection. Photo by Nadar; E. Bronte: National Portrait Gallery; Joseph Conrad: Mansell Collection; Charles Dickens: Photo: H. Watkins. Courtesy of Trustees of Dickens House; George Eliot: National Portrait Gallery and Nuneaton Public Library; E. M. Forster: P. N. Furbank; Thomas Hardy: L. Harrison Matthews; Henry James: Mansell Collection. Photo: E. Hoppé; James Joyce: National Library of Ireland. Photo: C. P. Curran; D. H. Lawrence: Radio Times Hulton Picture Library and courtesy of Witter Bynner; Tolstoy: APN Novosti; Turgenev: courtesy of D. Magarshack; Mark Twain: Bettman Archives and Brown Brothers; Virginia Woolf: Bettman Archives. Photo: Man Ray, and Culver Pictures Inc., Zola: Mansell Collection. Photo: Nadar.

The Nineteenth-century Novel and its Legacy

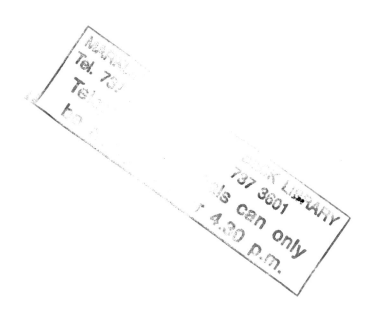